LIFE
ON THE
INSIDE

ONE CORRECTIONAL OFFICER'S STORY

JOHN B. WILLIAMS

Suite 300 - 990 Fort St
Victoria, BC, V8V 3K2
Canada

www.friesenpress.com

Copyright © 2020 by John B. Williams
First Edition — 2020

All rights reserved.

This is a story about my life; I have tried to recreate the events in my life, and the choices and challenges that I faced along the way, as well as the people that helped to shape my life.

No part of this publication may be reproduced in any form, or by any means, electronic or mechanical, including photocopying, recording, or any information browsing, storage, or retrieval system, without permission in writing from FriesenPress.

ISBN
978-1-5255-8535-7 (Hardcover)
978-1-5255-8536-4 (Paperback)
978-1-5255-8537-1 (eBook)

1. BIOGRAPHY & AUTOBIOGRAPHY, LAW ENFORCEMENT

Distributed to the trade by The Ingram Book Company

GLOSSARY

CMO: Case management officer.

CO: Correctional officer.

CX 1: A correctional officer.

CX 2: A Senior correctional officer.

CX 4: A Supervisor.

D/W: Deputy Warden or 2 I/C of the institution.

ETA: Escorted Temporary Absence. Usually for a medical or personal when an inmate is taken out of the institution.

IPSO: Institutional preventive security officer.

Keeper: Correctional supervisor, CX 5 or 6.

PC: Protective custody

Range: A large hallway in a cell block or living unit that contains cells.

Seg: Segregation, a secure unit where inmates are kept away from the general population inmates inside an institution.

SHU: Special handling unit, a highly secured unit for inmates who have committed a serious crime while under sentence.

UM: Unit manager.

UTA: Unescorted temporary absence, classed as a rehabilitation escort.

V&CO: Visits and Correspondence, the department responsible for all visitations and mail going in and out of a correctional institution.

CONTENTS

DEDICATION

This book is dedicated to Mr. and Mrs. Jack and Gloria Ross. If not for their intervention, I could have easily landed on the wrong side of the bars. They came into my life at a critical point and saw that I was a lost soul. It was through their wisdom, guidance, and support that set me on the most positive path of self-discovery.

I also dedicate this book to the many correctional officers, men and women alike, that I had the honour to work side by side with throughout my career in the Correctional Service of Canada.

ABOUT THE AUTHOR

Born in North Vancouver to Vern and Sandra Williams and the eldest of two children, John Williams grew up primarily in North Vancouver and Coquitlam, British Columbia.

He left school at the age of 17, and at 19 joined the Canadian Armed Forces. Following his discharge, he had varied employment in private security, eventually finding something where he excelled and enjoyed.

The journey was not an easy one.

"Every block of stone has a statue inside and it is the task of the sculptor to discover it. Michelangelo

At the early age of 21, the author found his rewarding career with the Penitentiary Service of Canada, in one of the most significant prisons in Canadian history: the British Columbia Penitentiary.

INTRODUCTION

It's taken me a few years to write this book, reflecting on my life, including my early years, to now sum up the experiences that affected me throughout my life. We all face choices, but sometimes the choice is right in front of you, and you can't see it. Along the way, people and events come into our lives for a reason presenting unique personal experiences.

It is via those relationships that I eventually found myself on a path of self-discovery.

Throughout my career as a correctional officer, I worked alongside such notorious inmates as murderer Andy Bruce, serial killer Clifford OLSON, predator and sexual psychopath John RITCEY (Headhunter), Wells Gray Provincial Park killer David SHEARING, and notorious sex offender (the Paper Bag Rapist) John Horace OUGHTON, just to name a few.

All transpired via numerous government changes, four different uniform changes, two riots, numerous murders, hangings, slashing's, and a dangerous hypodermic needle prick while searching an inmate's room. I worked at various security levels—maximum, medium, and minimum—as well as a Native healing lodge. In addition, I served three years as regional president of the newly founded Union of Correctional Officers (UCCO-SACC-CSN).

I am a Recipient of the Governor General's Corrections Exemplary Service Medal and Bar, and retired from the Correctional Service of Canada in 2013.

Prison life is very graphic and violent.
Some content of this book might not be suitable for some readers

CHAPTER 1

THE BEGINNING

Age 5

My sister Cindy, three years my junior, and I, were reared in a dysfunctional family. Our parents married young. Mother was 16 when I was born, and my father 21. What I remember most of my childhood is my parents fighting. I was in preschool when I recalled them arguing and escalating to the point where I had to take my sister Cindy into a storage area under the stairs. Our grandfather fixed up an old metal rocking horse and painted it like a pinto pony. I would put her on it with me and cover her ears, rocking her back and forth until our parents stopped yelling at one another.

I remember one day my mother sent me to school on a Saturday. I knew from her demeanour that she was in emotional stress, but did as I was told and went to school, with lunch in hand. I couldn't figure out why the doors were locked and banged on the door.

A janitor opened it asking me, "What can I do for you?"

I said, "My mother sent me to school today."

He laughed and said, "Today's Saturday." Then he spied my lunch box and asked, "So what do you have in there? Your lunch?"

I replied, "Yes," then naively handed him my lunch container, which he opened and helped himself to my sandwiches.

He finished them, saying, "Well, Sonny, time for you to go home, and thank your mother for me."

I went home crying, not because he had taken my lunch, but humiliated that my mother had sent me to school. When I arrived home, I yelled at my mother for sending me to school on a Saturday.

I didn't realize until I was a little older that it was not my mother's fault; she was upset from an argument the night before with my father.

My mother told me years later that I was not a typical child. During my young years, I was independent, stubborn, and rebellious to authority. She told me one story, which I have always remembered and laughed at on more than one occasion.

I was about five years old and we were living in Kitimat, BC. One day, I was being a bit of pest to my mother while she was caring for my toddler sister and trying to get some chores around the house. She came to the end of her wits and decided to put me in a harness. She felt I had to be tethered since I was a practised escape artist and, on numerous occasions, headed out into the world on my three-wheeler bike with my dog, Spot. This often forced my parents to call the police to report me missing.

That particular morning my mother put me in a harness and tethered me to a tree in our back yard. Nowadays, her actions could be considered child abuse, but this was her last resort since I was a handful at times.

My mother returned to the house, put my sister down for a nap and got some needed housework done, knowing that I was secured in the back yard. After a while, there was a knock at the door. My mother opened the door to find herself greeted by a policeman. The officer proceeded to say that they had received a call from one of the local neighbours, stating that there was a young boy hanging from a tree in the back yard of their neighbour's home. My mother, totally shocked by this news, immediately turned and ran to the back door; she opened it to find me hanging from in my harness from the tree that she had secured me too.

The neighbour observed me trying to climb the tree when I slipped; the rope got wrapped around a branch, thus leaving me hanging off the ground in my harness. Nothing ever came of my little antic. Mother never tied me to that tree ever again.

My parents eventually separated when I was around six years old. I remember that day when my father, grandmother, and two uncles were helping pack up our apartment. I couldn't understand why our mother was not there and recall asking where she was. Grandmother told me, "She is at work, Johnny. It's okay and everything will be fine."

I can only imagine what my mother felt that day when she arrived home, opening the door to an empty apartment—no kids or husband—only to find her remaining personal belongings scattered around the rooms and closets.

Cindy and I were then placed in our grandparents' four-bedroom North Vancouver home. The house was designed and built by my grandfather and based on typical English architecture.

It was one of four houses on the street that was surrounded on three sides by trees. At the end of our driveway was a blocked off road that led up the hill to a nearby quarry, which made for hours of adventurous play and entertaining fun. Cindy and I and the local kids enjoyed childhood there in the years that followed.

My grandmother was of German descent born February 6, 1910. She was a short, overweight woman who did her best to look after the family and home while working full-time during the day as a chamber maid at one of the local hotels in North Vancouver. I have memories of her coming home from work occasionally smelling of beer and a little bit tipsy as she tried to hug and kiss me.

Uncle David was the oldest of the three brothers, and was at the time living full-time with my grandparents. My grandparents pulled him out from school because of some medical condition. I never really did find out what it was that he had. He was an averaged size, soft-spoken man, who would be best described as my grandmother's house boy. He cooked and cleaned around the house, and was tasked with the responsibility of looking after Cindy and I when everyone was away at work.

My other uncle, Uncle Raymond, was the middle of the three brothers and was living on his own at the time. He was best being described as the character of Fonzie on *Happy Days*. I remember him dressed in tight-fitting black jeans and biker-style black leather jacket with his coal-black hair slicked back in ultimate greaser style. He was the rebel and bad boy of the family. I always admired how he stated his own opinions, voicing whatever was on his mind.

My grandfather was a kind gentleman who was born in Sussex, England, on November 20, 1900. He met my grandmother when he arrived in Ontario via steamship. He had served in the military in the infantry during WW II, but ever talked about his experiences. He was in his late 60s at the time, slim and tall, much like my father. He was head of the household when one was needed, a lover of the arts and music. Naturally creative with his hands, he enjoyed watercolour painting. Evenings were spent listening to music and painting, or working in his wood shop. During the day, he was a gardener for elite East Vancouver homes.

One cherished memory of him as a child was when I used to wake up early on cool mornings, and sneak downstairs into his room. (My grandparents never slept together up as long as I could remember.) Crawling into his warm bed was the epitome of feeling safe, comfortable, and secure. Grandfather had the scent of analgesic balm that he used for his sore joints and that smell to this day makes me smile, bringing back fond memories.

One evening, he was relaxing listening to music from such composers such as Beethoven, Tchaikovsky, and Brahms. I remember him telling me the story of when he was on the stern of the ship that brought him to Ontario, Canada. He was rolling a cigarette and when he looked up, he saw a periscope pop up out of the water not far behind the stern of the ship. He knew that the waters they were in were patrolled by the Nazi U-boats, and he truly believed that the only reason that they did not sink them was the simple fact that the ship was Canadian, and flying the Canadian flag astern.

This remarkable man used to tell me stories of when he was in charge of the gardens and grounds of Windsor Castle. He showed some old black and white pictures of him playing tennis with the Duke of Windsor, Edward the VIII. He also said that he taught Edward's children how to play the piano, since he learned to play at an early age. Time is often unkind as he was later stricken with arthritis in his hands and could no longer enjoy his greatest love in life.

★   ★   ★

A nasty custody battle occurred between my parents and this battle didn't end with us moving to our grandparents' house.

It was a warm summer day and Cindy and I were playing out on the front lawn of our grandparents' home. I could see my mother leaning out the passenger window of a car and waving to us. The car pulled into the driveway alongside the house and our mother got out of the car and rushed over to us. The next thing I remember is my grandmother yelling, "Johnny! You and Cindy get back in the house!" while she was running towards us.

My mother grabbed my sister by the arm, trying to get her into the car. Grandmother, seeing this, reached out and grabbed my sister by her other arm. They were pulling her back and forth in some tug of war game until my sister screamed out in pain. My mother automatically let my sister go. I still can remember the shock and painfully torn look on my mother's face as tears ran down her cheeks, watching my grandmother drag each of us by the arm back to the house.

Once inside, I could hear my mother yelling outside. All she wanted was to see her children. My grandmother ordered my uncle David to take Cindy and I both upstairs to his room. Uncle David's room looked over the driveway with a large double glass window that was open. I watched and heard my mother and grandmother arguing loudly.

Uncle David ordered Cindy and I into a wardrobe that was in his room, closing the door and ordering us, "Don't you dare come out until I tell you to." My sister was crying and I did my best to try to calm her down. I could see through the crack between the doors. Uncle David stood by the open window with a rifle in his hands. He aimed it out the window, yelling at my mother, "Just leave and go away." I could hear screams of fear coming from my mother and a man's voice saying, "Sandy, we have to go now." Next was the sound of car doors closing, the racing of an engine, and then a car sped away.

I never forgot what my uncle David did that day. It created distance between us up until he passed away from cancer. I visited him in the hospital the day before he died and told him how I felt those many years ago. I understood later that it was just his way of protecting Cindy and I, and I forgave him.

After the wardrobe and shotgun incident, the police investigated. Subsequently, my sister and I were removed from our grandparents' home and placed in foster care to wait a court decision as to which parent would get custody of us.

As it turned out, my mom was a single and working five days a week at a drug store in downtown Vancouver and the judge felt that my father could provide a more stable family environment, living with my grandparents and our uncle David as our home guardian.

Cindy and I remained living in North Vancouver for six years and then relocated to Coquitlam after my grandfather invested money in the stock market. He lost everything.

Over the next few years, Cindy habitually ran away to be with our mother, who had remarried and was living in North Vancouver at the time. My father, finally at his wits' end, signed over custody of Cindy to my mother.

I remained with my father, grandparents, and Uncle David. During these the years, my father had a habit of slapping me in the back of the head when he was upset with me for something that I had done.

One day, we were attending a Christmas party held by my father's employers. We were about to leave when my father noticed that my sister was off somewhere visiting. He stood up and said, "Let's go find your sister."

I don't remember what I said, but I'm sure it didn't please him. He looked at me and raised his hand threateningly to give me a whack to the back of the head. As soon as he raised his hand, I dropped to my knees. He stopped for a second, looked up, and noticed people watching. I will always remember the look on his face: total shock. He then lowered his hand, leaned down, and picked me up by the arm, saying, "Let's go. I see your sister."

He never hit me again after that day. My father and I remained living with my grandparents up until my father remarried when I turned 15. My new stepmother boarded a few horses in a field next to where my father worked and never had kids of her own. I found out later in life she did not have a good childhood and that had a bearing on our relationship.

The next few years were touch and go. I was a stubborn, rebellious kid with anger issues. It didn't help that my stepmother and I did not get along at all when my father was not around. She, however, did the best she could with a difficult situation. My father and she were at their wits' end with my anger and rebellious issues, ending up going as far as taking me to a psychiatrist to deal with my emotional issues. We both attended appointments once every month in hopes to curve my rebellious mannerisms and angry temperament.

No avail. All was kept bottled up inside for years to come. I would eventually learn how to control these traits and heal my emotional scars with time and transcendental meditation.

I will always honour my stepmother for the many years she devoted to looking after my family when they were sick or ill. She was highly supportive and was always faithfully at my father's side after he was diagnosed with terminal cancer in spring of 1995. He passed away gracefully at their home at the early age of 60.

My 16th birthday

SCHOOL OF HARD KNOCKS

My days in school were rough. I was a magnet for the school bullies. In retrospect, my geeky appearance probably didn't help matters much.

It all started when I was in grade five and was living with my grandparents in North Vancouver.

My school was about two blocks from home, less if I took the shortcut through the trees. Three boys in my school took particular pleasure bullying me every chance they got. They would knock my books out of my arms as they passed me by in the halls or shove me into the lockers when no teacher was around.

One day, I was taking the shortcut to home. They were hiding in wait for me to come along, jumped out in front of me, circled me, and the biggest one of the three knocked my books out of my hand. They then started to push and shove me between the three of them, cursing and calling me names. I tried to push one of them back, which only resulted my getting hit in the face. When they finally tired of me, I grabbed my books and ran for home as fast as my legs could carry me.

When I walked through the door, my grandmother took one look at me, all battered and beaten, and became frantic. She asked me what happened, but I just looked down and told her I got beaten up on my way home. She gave me a hug, then asked if I was okay or hurt. I could only tell her that my eye hurt a lot. That developed into one hell of a shiner the next day.

My grandmother called my dad at work, telling him what had happened. When he got home that evening, he announced we were going to go to my school for an appointment to meet the principal. When we arrived at my school and met with the principal, the first thing said was an apology to my father and I, also relating he was unaware how bad the bullying was.

After this, things quieted down somewhat and a few short years later we moved to Coquitlam and to a new school.

HIGH SCHOOL SENIOR YEARS

In grade nine, it all turned for the worse yet again. Unfortunately, I was not one of those kids who could fade into the background school population.

Long blond hair, wire-framed glasses, and being a few pounds overweight all made me kind of obvious.

My low self-esteem and insecurity issues led me to reason perhaps that was why I was the kid that school bullies targeted. No matter how hard I tried to keep my head down and hide in the shadows, I struggled constantly to be unnoticeable.

I remember one group of kids who enjoyed picking on me. Their ringleader challenged me to a fight after school to take place in Blue Mountain, a hangout park next to our school. It seemed the whole school showed up to watch the fight. I had no experience at fighting but remember my friends telling me that I needed to stand up to this guy and that it was crucial for me to get in the first punch to win.

We squared off and he came at me like a bull. Before I could get my hands up, he punched me in the head and the next thing I knew I was lying on the ground. He started to kick me in the stomach as I lay there, dazed and confused. The next thing I knew, he was being dragged off by some of the kids from school, while a few others were helping me to my feet. As fast as it happened it was over and while the crowd was dispensing, I could hear that bastard yelling, "What the hell! I won the fight! Where's everyone going?" No one supported the bully.

In 1975, I dropped out of high school before finishing grade 11. I was a troubled teen who was rebellious, full of anger and rage. I turned to numerous street drugs of the seventies: marijuana, acid, and MDA (methylenedioxyamphetamine). I was in freefall, with no job, a basic grade 10 education, and hopelessly mixed-up, confused, and angry. I knew I was in a bad space but still kept digging myself deeper into a dark abyss of shame, despair, and non-existent self-worth. I had no concept of what I was going to do with my life.

As I stated earlier, my stepmom and I were seeing a psychiatrist together. The doctor, hoping to curb my acts of anger and rage, prescribed valium.

I remember an incident where I totally lost control of myself. I was driving an old Rambler car; the starter would not engage sometimes, and I would have to hit it with something. I had a job interview appointment that morning and was running late. I got into my car and turned the key, but it didn't start.

I reached in the back seat to find the ice pick my grandfather gave me to chip the ice off our front steps of our house. I got out of the car, opened the hood, and gave the starter a few taps with the ice pick, then turned the key again. No go.

I picked up the pick again and hit the starter two or three more times. Feeling the rage swelling inside me. I tried it one last time and when it didn't work, I slammed the hood down, grabbed the ice pick, and repeatedly swung it over my head and into the hood of my car, then through the front window. I kept smashing the car with everything that I had, fuelled by rage and anger, continuing this until completely exhausted.

I tossed the ice pick into the back seat and returned to the house.

My father was standing in the doorway having watched me all along. As I was coming up the stairs, he calmly asked, "So, did that fix it?"

I looked at him with still-unbridled rage taking him by surprise. He backed away into the house as I stomped off to my bedroom, slamming the door behind me. I stayed in my room for seemed like a few hours until my father knocked on the door, asking, "Is it safe to come in? You know I'll have to call a wrecker to tow your car away?"

I said, "Fine, it's a piece of junk anyways."

He didn't say much after that, but I could sense that he was a little concerned about my rash behaviour. I thanked him and headed out the door but before I left, I called a friend. I needed to get away and find something to calm me down. Abusing drugs and alcohol was my means to escape and hope to control my rage and temper. Now I know it only made it worse, but I couldn't see it at that time. "Classic."

Later in the day I scored a hit of acid and enjoyed a few beers at a local bar before heading home. I took the LSD just before leaving the bar.

I knew the drug usually lasted about 12 hours, so when I arrived at home around ten that night, my father and stepmom were in bed as they had to be up early for work in Vancouver.

I remember I was feeling pretty good, enjoying the artificial mellowness of the drug. I crawled into bed and didn't realize how stoned I was until I started to hallucinate and noticed the wallpaper in my room starting to peel off the walls. I'm not sure if I nodded off, but the next thing I knew my stepmother was knocking on my door. As usual, she just walked in.

"Good morning! This is a good day to get out and find yourself a job."

It was still dark outside, so she leaned down and turned on the lamp next to my bed. The sudden flash of light in my eyes caused me extreme pain. I just closed my eyes and as soon as she left, leaned over and killed the light.

Fifteen minutes later she came back into my room, turned the light back on, and said, "Get your ass out of bed. You are going to go find a job today."

She slammed my door and left. I got out of bed, feeling a little light-headed, and headed down the hallway to the bathroom. Once inside, I closed the door behind me and then looked into the mirror. My pupils were dilated and my mouth was as dry as dirt. I was still stoned.

I brushed my teeth, trying to waste as much time as I could to avoid looking either one of them in the eye. I heard the front door close and, thinking they had left and the coast was clear to come out, I headed to the kitchen.

My stepmother was still there.

I dropped my eyes to the floor pretending I was just waking up.

"I left the eggs and milk out so you can make yourself some scrambled eggs" she said, and then reached up to the cupboard above the stove and took down my valium. Now I knew where it was hidden—hidden for good reason.

The frying pan was on the stove, I grabbed the milk pouring some into the frying pan while she handed me my daily two pills of valium.

She started to laugh, saying, "You must still be asleep; you forgot to put the eggs in."

I laughed, reached over, grabbed three eggs, and cracked them into the frying pan.

As she headed out the door, she said, "Hope you have a good day," and was gone.

I immediately turned off the stove and took a deep breath. There was no way I was going anywhere in my condition. I grabbed a cup of coffee, went into the living room, and turned on my father's pride and joy stereo. I was not allowed to touch it.

I found the good rock and roll channel, cranked up the sound and sat back in his chair in full vegged out mode. I started to come down from my high but didn't want to crash. My mind wandered to where the valium was hidden. I got up from my father's chair, and headed to the kitchen, and reached into the cupboard above the stove. I noticed a few receipt books, moved them around and just behind one, found my bottle of pills.

I can't remember how many were left, but remember taking about half a dozen. I downed the pills with another coffee and headed back to the living room and stretched out on the couch listening to the sound of the base beating out of the speakers.

I passed out.

Next thing I remember is my stepmother trying to shake me awake and me hearing loud static sounds coming out of my dad's stereo. I opened my eyes and heard my stepmother's voice, saying, "Oh my God, you're stoned! Just wait 'til your father gets home!"

I got up from the couch staggering my way down what appeared to be a long hallway, which in reality was only 12 steps. Once in my room and behind my closed bedroom door, I crashed on my bed.

A short time later, my father knocked and came in to see me lying face up on my bed. With a worried expression he asked, "Are you going to be okay?"

I told him, "Yes, Dad. I will be fine."

He knelt next to me on the bed with his hand on my shoulder and said, "Okay, get some rest, my son. If you're hungry, I'll get you something to eat." He stood up, then smiled at me saying, "I'll check up on you later," and left.

I then overheard my stepmother telling Dad she found the empty pill bottle on the kitchen table, and was concerned that maybe they should take me to the hospital.

The next morning, I woke up to an empty house since they went to work. I was surprised but relieved. I was not looking forward to that father-son talk.

Still feeling rather spaced out, I was sitting at the kitchen table watching TV with a bowl of cereal. A commercial came on about the Canadian Armed Forces. The message was about getting an education and seeing the world.

It was at that moment that I had my epiphany. That life-defining moment came over me, and suddenly that was the plan.

I was going to join the Canadian Armed Forces. I knew I needed a drastic change. I was not coping well with my drug use, my family situation, and everything else. I said to myself, "What the hell. Why not?"

I got showered and dressed and headed out of the house to the nearest bus stop. In a short while, I was standing at the front doors of the Canadian

Armed Forces Recruitment Centre in downtown Vancouver. I took a deep breath, reached out, grabbed the doorknob, and walked in. Standing behind the counter was a middle-aged gentleman in uniform. He greeted me with a big smile, and asked what he could do for me. I automatically stuck my hand out and said, "I would like to join the Canadian Armed Forces, Sir."

He reached out and shook my hand and proceeded to tell me all the advantages of signing up.

Looking back now, it was probably the best thing I could have ever done for myself and I often wonder where I would be today if I had not made that decision. We chatted for a bit and the next thing I knew he had me filling out an aptitude test, to see what my strengths and weakness were and what position I would be best qualified for.

We learned there were three areas that were best suited for me. First one was a Medical Technician, second was Military Police, and third was a cook. I didn't have any genuine interest being a Field Medic, and knowing I had authority issues that had to deal with, I chose to be a cook. That could be a viable vocation if I was not in the military.

When I arrived home later that evening, my dad and stepmom were home. I sat down at the kitchen table as my stepmother was preparing dinner, and she said pleasantly, "Hope you're hungry." I didn't realize it until that moment that I had not eaten all day; I was ravenous.

Dad came to the table, sat down, and asked what I had been up too during the day. Before I could answer, he carried on about me taking all my medication and that I had blown up the speaker to his stereo.

Just when he was going to talk about something else, I interrupted him. "I have something to tell you. I went to Vancouver today and enlisted in the Canadian Armed Forces." I then produced my leave slip, which stated I was on leave for five days and would be flying out to basic training in Nova Scotia within the week.

Well, you should have seen the look on their faces. Both were speechless for a few minutes.

My dad said, "What in the hell inspired you to do that? You're a fool and you have no idea of what you're getting yourself into!"

My reply was that we were currently not at war with anyone and that Canadian Armed Forces were mainly Peacekeeping duties in other countries.

I had signed up for three years, after which I could leave or sign up for another three years. I went on to tell them that that I signed up to be a cook and I could be posted anywhere.

My stepmother surprised me when she said, "Well, it's a good thing that you took something on that you'll benefit from when you get out."

They knew that it was all set and done, and there was nothing that they could do or say that would change my mind.

CHAPTER 2

THE CANADIAN ARMED FORCES

I enlisted in the Canadian Armed Forces on February 29, 1975. Two weeks later, five of my closest friends drove me to Vancouver International Airport, where I boarded an Air Canada jet to Nova Scotia for basic training. I arrived in Cornwallis, Nova Scotia, in March 1975. It was damn cold, and snow was in the air. I was on a bus full of other long-haired hippie-looking recruits, who were much like me. Everyone was pretty quiet when we pulled up to the barracks where we would live for the next four months.

We all filed out of the bus and were instructed to line up outside our new home for roll call; then we were instructed to grab our gear and take it into the building where we were given our cot assignments.

BASIC TRAINING WAS HARD

I was not in the greatest physical shape and we went running every morning. The regimen of inspections, drill, courses on military protocol, and hand to hand combat became something that I started to enjoy. And an added bonus was the comradeship with my fellow cadets.

I grew close to a guy named John Bear, an Aboriginal from Manitoba. We got into mischief once in a while, but all in good fun. There were events that happened in barracks that educated and defined me. One evening some of my fellow recruits were able to get their hands on a few bottles of vodka. Of course, drinking in the barracks was a huge no-no, and anyone caught faced serious discipline charges.

The next morning at 0600, we received a surprise inspection. Two corporals were yelling at us to get our lazy asses out of bed, get dressed, make our beds, and stand at attention. If you were the last one standing, you would be doing extra chores, like washing the bathroom floor with only a toothbrush. I know. I was one of them.

We were all standing at attention at the foot of our beds. I know in the movies they talk about bouncing a coin off your bed when it is made properly. No joke, it really happens, and if was not made right, there were consequences—like the corporal literally tearing your closet and foot locker apart, and then ordering you to put it back in order perfectly.

During inspection, one of the corporals found one of the half empty vodka bottles hidden behind a recruit's locker. His voice thundered, "Oh, now it would appear that this squad of low-life half-wits had some fun last night!"

The recruit who tried to hide the bottle was ordered to take two steps forward and remain standing at attention. The corporal then proceeded to pace up and down each side of the barracks saying that all of us would do extra duties if someone did not speak up and tell him who was involved in the little party the previous night.

I was not fond of cleaning bathrooms with a toothbrush and since I did not partake in drinking that night, took a deep breath, took one step forward, and remained at attention. A hush came over the barracks, our instructors ordered everyone to remain at attention, and I was then escorted to their office.

That was the first big mistake of my military life. "Huge."

Sparing the reader details of what happened next, I will say I got the cold shoulder from every recruit in my squad, and still had to scrub toilets with a tooth brush every day for a week.

That evening we were all tucked in our bunks for the night, I received my first and only "blanket party." They waited until I was asleep, then covered me with a blanket and beat me with wooden coat hangers. When it was over, I was told to not move and not say a word to anyone. I woke the next morning sore and stiff, and from that day forward, things slowly got better. I was eventually once again accepted into the squad.

A blanket party is a form of corporal punishment or hazing within the military or military academies aptly demonstrated in a scene from *Full Metal Jacket*. The victim's head and body are covered with a blanket as to prevent him/her from fighting back and or identifying their assailants. They are basically used to bring a barracks bully into line or to correct an infraction of the squad rules.

From then on, I gave basic training everything that I had. I pushed myself to exhaustion, slaved day and night, making sure my teeth were reflected in mirror-polished boots and my dress and deportment were of the highest quality.

I wanted to "be the best that I could be" even though it sounds like the recruitment cliché, I was completely focused.

When we graduated basic training, I was a given the honour of flag carrier for our squad. This prestigious recognition is only given to recruits who achieved the highest ratings within their squad.

After graduation, I flew home for a week before reporting to the military base in Borden, Ontario, for my cooking course.

Basic Training Course, Cornwallis, Nova Scotia.

When I arrived at Vancouver International Airport, my high school friends picked me up and once in the car, a paper-covered bottle was immediately passed to me. I was bragging about how I could drink them under the table now. Well, that didn't happen, and we eventually landed at a close friend's parents' home and partied the whole evening. I woke the next morning with a huge hangover, showered and got dressed in my uniform.

One of my best friends, Daryl, drove me to my parents' home in Maple Ridge and dropped me off in front of the house. My father and I had not communicated much since I left home for basic training, other than a few letters. I took a deep breath and I walked up to the front door with an uneasy stomach, no doubt because of too much alcohol the night before and being nervous, not knowing what to expect. I banged three times on the door.

I heard his heavy footsteps, and then the door opened. Our eyes met, and as he looked me up and down, for the first time in my life, I saw tears running down his cheeks. He reached out and grabbed me and hugged me so hard I almost couldn't breathe.

I spent the next few days staying with my dad and stepmother, talking about my adventures in basic training and where I wanted to be posted after competing my cook's course in Barry, Ontario. I told them that I had put in for two choices: the first one was Canadian Forces Base Chilliwack. The second was Canadian Forces Base Esquimalt: Canada's Pacific coast naval base and home to Port Maritime Forces Pacific.

My basic military training roused passions to explore what life was all about. Prior to me flying home to Vancouver, I flew out of Ontario via Nova Scotia, and while sitting in the lounge outside my gate, I gazed out the window at my plane. It was a 747 and about the biggest thing that I have ever seen in my life. Shortly, we were called for boarding. I didn't realize I was flying first class home. Dressed in my uniform, I walked onto the plane and the stewardess smiled at me as I gave her my boarding pass. She showed me the privileged seat and aisle, saying, "Thank you, Sir. I hope you enjoy the flight."

It was like someone slapped me in the face. Sir! Wow. I had never been called that in my life. I was overwhelmed by this respect for the entire flight's duration. I really liked it.

NELLIE'S BLOCK

I took my cook training at Canadian Forces Base Borden and after three months was posted to Canadian Forces Base Esquimalt and assigned to what they called Nellie's Block.

It was the main mess hall for all junior rank military personnel working and residing on the base. During the summer months, it catered to up to 150 regular military personnel and another 100 or more reservists. I came to enjoy cooking working with a great bunch of guys and gals. I never had to mop floors, do dishes, or pots and pans. It was a great job, although I was not too fond of getting up at 0400 to open and start up the kitchen.

Six months passed quickly. One morning, after the breakfast line, a few of my fellow cooks and myself were having coffee in the dining room when my warrant officer called out from his office, "Williams! Front and centre!"

I reported to his office, he looked up from his desk and invited me in. "Well, Mr. Williams, I am giving you the afternoon off today."

I guess I looked as if I did something wrong, but didn't want to ask.

He looked up at me and started to laugh, then said, "Congratulations son, you have been assigned to the *HMCS Gatineau*. You need to put your affairs in order and report to your ship at 0800 hours tomorrow."

Graduation

HMCS GATINEAU

I was going to be on a destroyer. The thought was a little scary, but also exciting. I thanked him for the news. He handed me my transfer papers, and reached out and shook my hand. I rushed up to my room to pack. I reported to my ship at 0745 the next morning.

I remember standing at the foot of the brow (a gangway from ship to shore when the ship is tied up in port), looking at the size of my ship, and being very impressed. Her captain was a man whom I would come to highly respect, Lieutenant Commander John Charles Slade.

I walked up the brow onto the quarterdeck and saluted; I stepped onto my new home, and was greeted by the warrant officer on duty. (Saluting the quarterdeck is a Navy tradition. any sailor entering or departing the quarterdeck is to salute; it is seen as respecting the authority of the ship and the colours that are flown on the quarterdeck.)

"Permission to come aboard."

The warrant officer looked me up and down and asked, "What's your business here, sailor?"

I handed him my papers, after a few minutes looked up at me and said, "Welcome aboard."

The warrant officer on deck directed me to sign in, and said that someone would come up and take below and get me settled. A few minutes later a man dressed in cook's whites met me on the quarterdeck. He was a big, stocky man. He walked up to me and shook my hand, then said, "I am Petty Officer Stevens, son. You will be working under my command and welcome aboard the *Gatineau*. I will take you down and get you settled and introduce you to your new home."

SNOWBALL

Junior rank cooks were generally bunked in the bow of the ship. Petty Officer Stevens was an experienced sailor and cook, and had been on the *HMCS Gatineau* for about five years. His gruff manner and honesty were a pleasant change from my previous warrant officer, and I enjoyed his sense of humour. He introduced me to another new cook who was assigned to the Gatineau, who introduced himself and said, "They call me Snowball." I can understand why. He was a stocky guy around the same age as me, and earned his nick-name due to the simple fact that when he was in his whites, he resembled a snowball. He was assigned the bunk above me, and over the next few months, I found myself not liking him very much; he was arrogant, and thought he knew everything about anything. I remember a few incidents when I just wanted to throw his ass overboard.

One particular incident occurred when we were assigned to open the galley in the morning. He was not a morning person, and I always wondered how the hell he got through basic training, and wondered how many blanket parties he had. I woke up around 0430 hrs, went and showed, and got dressed in my whites. I gave Snowball a nudge to wake him, and said I was going to go and set up the galley. "Get your butt out of bed." He mumbled something, but I ignored him and was more focused on getting the galley ready for morning breakfast. I reported to the galley at 0500 hours, and fired up the steam table, and turned on the grills and started to lay everything out for the morning line. This usually consisted of baked beans, stewed tomatoes, bacon, and hash brown potatoes.

I pulled out the mashed potatoes out from the previous night and four cookie sheets of pre-laid-out bacon from the night before, as instructed by Petty Officer Stevens, I turned on the ovens and placed them inside, and then turned on the grills. I looked down at my watch and was ahead of myself, but Snowball had not shown up yet, so I returned to our quarters to find him still sleeping in his bunk. I gave him another shake and said, "Get your ass out of bed Snowball. I am almost ready for the morning line."

He mumbled, "Where is my tea"?

Apparently Petty Officer Stevens had been spoiling Snowball by doing exactly the same thing while getting the galley prepared and then, unknown to me, would bring him a cup of tea and place it on his chest; thus, if he didn't get up, he would eventually spill the tea on himself, getting his lazy ass out of bed. Well, I was in no mood to babysit this guy, and said, "You either get your ass out of your bunk, or I will help you get out of it."

He rolled over on his side, facing away from me, and said, "Go get my tea, asshole."

Well that was it. I'd had enough of this idiot and was not going to cater to him. I stepped up to his bunk, reached over him, grabbed the bottom sheet of his bed, and with everything that I had, rolled him out of his bunk. He hit the floor with a loud thud and rolled on his side. Seeing that we shared our quarters with other cooks and stewards, it didn't take long to wake everyone up.

Snowball staggered to his feet and tried to give me a shove, but I stepped aside just as one of the stewards stepped in and separated us. The steward standing between us told me to report back to the galley, and then turned to Snowball and said, "I would highly recommend that you go get showered and report to work, or you leave me no choice but to report your actions to Petty Officer Stevens."

I turned and left as Snowball headed off to the head to showered and get dressed. Nothing was reported, but Snowball was never late for work again, and a few weeks later he was reassigned to Nellie's Block on the base.

I enjoyed my time aboard *HMCS Gatineau*; it was great being out at sea. I remember one time we were doing manoeuvres outside Seattle a few months later with the US Navy. It was an awesome sight seeing the size of their fleet. I remember we were cruising next to an aircraft carrier called *Enterprise*. I remember looking up at her first deck, which was three stories off the water. She was a sight to see, and even in heavy seas, she seemed to move through the water with such ease.

HCMS Gatineau

HMCS Gatineau was a Restigouche-class destroyer in the Royal Canadian Navy and later the Canadian Forces during the Cold War, from 1959 to 1996. She was the third ship in her class and the second vessel to carry the designation *HCMS Gatineau*. Her complement was 249; she was eventually sold for scrap metal in 2009.

While assigned to the *HMCS Gatineau*, I was in constant contact with my mother who was now married to a gentleman by the name of Johnny Clarke. He was a large man with a deep, commanding voice, and an air of authority about him. A kind man, he always treated Cindy and I with love and respect. I came to call him Uncle John, as I was not comfortable calling him Dad, and he was just fine with that. During my time in the Navy, we became close and always kept in contact.

Uncle John told me that he had served in the Merchant Navy. (They were considered a fourth branch of the Canadian military alongside the Royal Canadian Navy, Canadian Army, and the Royal Canadian Air Force, and suffered the highest casualty rate of the four during the war.)

He was at the time employed as a representative of the Hotel Restaurant Bartender Union local based out of Vancouver, and had been for a number of years.

I recall him talking about how proud he was of me for joining the Navy.

UN HABITAT

In 1976, Vancouver, BC, held the UN Habitat: United Nations Conference on Human Settlements. Three ships were assigned to Vancouver for security reasons; the *Gatineau* was among one of those three.

I had called my mother and let her know that I would be in Vancouver for a week, and would have some leave time. My ship was safely secured at the Vancouver harbour docks two days before the UN Habitat. I called my mother the night before I arrived, she informed me that Uncle John would meet me at the docks and will bring me out to the house for dinner that evening.

We arrived around noon the next day. Once the ship was secured, those of us who were allowed to leave the ship departed. I was walking down the brow when I saw Uncle John standing next to his new car, a yellow and black 1973

Mach 1 Mustang, I remember what a sweet-looking car it was. I also noted however that he was not alone; he was in the company of two attractive women and his best friend Don, who was a bartender at the Army Navy Air Force Club in downtown Vancouver, where Uncle John was president of the club at the time. He wanted to come aboard and check out the ship. I looked at him with a puzzled look, and he said, "Not to worry. I brought the women for the boys." I had no idea of what he meant by that until later that evening.

I signed them all in, and escorted them down the junior ranks mess hall, where we had a small bar and beer machine. Beer at that time was 25 cents a bottle, and liquor was 15 cents a shot. We grabbed a table in the pig peg, which was a small private lounge next to the bar, located in the corner of the mess. The mess was about half full of my shipmates.

There was a bell hanging on a wall next to our table. Uncle John reached up, and grabbed the tail of the bell, and rang it three times, which meant a round on the house. There was an automatic roar of whooping sounds from my shipmates that echoed through the mess. Uncle John then reached into his pocket, pulled out a ball of bills, and threw a couple of hundred-dollar bills on the table. "A round on the house for the men of the *Gatineau*." Within minutes, the mess was packed with sailors, as a small swarm of my fellow shipmates had joined us. We spent a few hours on ship, and Uncle John bought half a dozen rounds for my shipmates. He looked at me and said, "We should go. I have a few things to do before we head home."

I said, "Okay, but what about the ladies you brought?"

He laughed and said, "I brought them as entertainment for the boys." When you bring guests aboard a ship you have to sign them in on the quarterdeck; thus, you are responsible to escort them on and off the ship. I, however, had no problem finding a few of my fellow shipmates to step up to volunteer to sign them in so they could stay aboard.

Uncle John, Don, and I headed off the ship. We were walking towards Uncle John's car when he handed me his keys and said, "You're driving."

I was absolutely thrilled to bits to get to drive his car; it was an impressive vehicle, and I remember reading about how fast it was for a stock car. So, I climbed in, started the car, and could feel the power under the hood. The first order of business was to drop Don off at the Army Navy Air Force Club, as he had to work the bar that evening.

The next stop was a hotel on Hastings Street. Uncle John was not a small man—stout with a bit of a belly—and at the time he was wearing a black sweater and sports jacket. When we pulled up to the front of the hotel, I could see what appeared to be the butt of a revolver tucked in his pants, under his sweater.

He opened the door, stepped out and, leaning back in, said, "Keep the car running. I'll be right back."

Well. I had no idea of what was going on. Thoughts were racing through my mind as to what was going to happen. He was only gone a short time. When he got back into the car, I automatically looked to see if he still had the gun with him, but I didn't see it. I gave out a big sigh of relief as he told me that we would be heading back to the Army Navy Air Force Club.

He had been president of the club for some ten years. I found later that no one ever ran against him.

We pulled up to the club, where he had his own designated parking spot behind the club. We got out and he said, "Open the trunk. I have a few things that I need to drop off."

I did as he asked. There were three or four paper bags, the ones with string handles on them, in the trunk. He grabbed them and said, "Okay, let's go." We entered the club through the back door and walked into the bar area. It was rather busy, with mostly naval personnel; he looked around and started heading towards some tables with his paper bags in hand.

I looked around and decided to belly up to the bar for a beer. Don was behind the bar, and said, "Beer's on the house to you any time you're here." He and my uncle John were pretty close friends, and I had met him on more than one occasion. He looked as if he had a few drinks himself while working. So, we chatted for a bit while I sipped my beer.

I took a moment to look around for Uncle John when this cute little woman a little younger than me walked up to me and said, "So I take it you're here off the boats."

"Yes, but I'm with my stepdad," I said and pointed in his direction.

She looked over where I was pointing and said in a rather surprised voice, "Oh, you must be Johnny Clarke's son. He talks about you all the time."

Surprised, I said, "Oh, really? Well, we should grab a table."

She said, "Sure."

We found one near the back of the bar, which was semi-quiet, and chatted about my time in the Navy. When Uncle John and Don came over and joined us, Uncle John said, "Oh, I see you've met BJ."

"Yes," I said.

Then he looked over at BJ and said, "BJ, how do you feel about giving my son a blow job?"

Well, I was shocked and just wanted to crawl under the table, but kept my composure.

Without blinking an eye, she said, "Well, Johnny, that's up to your son."

Don had his head down, resting on his arms on the table, and then raised himself up and said, "Hell, I'll pay for it."

She looked at me and said, "I think it will be my pleasure to look after the son of Johnny Clarke."

I finished my beer, and Uncle John was looking at his watch. "Shit," he said. "We're late; your mom is going to be pissed." So off we went, with BJ in tow.

My mom and Uncle John lived in a large five-bedroom home in Port Coquitlam; it was tucked away at the end of a street and was semi-isolated from nearby neighbours. We pulled into the roundabout driveway, I parked the car, and we all proceeded into the house. The entrance had large double doors and marble floor as you entered. The first thing you saw was an elegant staircase that led to the second floor. To the right was a door that opened to a large entertainment room equipped with a very large, well-stocked bar, pretty much the size of a small pub bar. Uncle John always liked to entertain his friends and co-workers, and had it fully stocked with everything you can imagine.

Mom came down the stairs to greet me, she was as elegant as she was beautiful. She walked across the hall and gave me a big hug and a kiss on my cheek. Then she looked over in Uncle John's direction, not too happy that we were late for dinner. I did my best to cover for him. She just shook it off and said, "Can you please take your guest into the bar and get her a drink?" Then she turned to Uncle John and said, "Johnny, a word," and headed back up the staircase.

I escorted BJ into the entertainment room and asked her what she would like. "Double vodka," was her response. After pouring the first one, she threw it back in one gulp and said, "Could I have another, please?"

So I poured her another, and then heard my mom calling out my name. I excused myself and said, "I will be right back," and left the room, closing the door behind me.

My mom was standing at the foot of the staircase. She handed me the keys to Uncle Johnny's car and said, "I need you to get that hooker out of my house, and take her back to Vancouver where she belongs. I'm not mad at you. I know missing dinner was not your fault, so keep the car till tomorrow, and be here in the morning for breakfast."

With that said, I told BJ that we were leaving, and out the door we went. I went back to my ship that night after dropping BJ off at home, and returned to my mother's for breakfast. Uncle John was pretty quiet over breakfast, but he knew that when my mother was upset, it would be best just not to speak too much, so as not to hit a nerve. He drove me back to my ship that afternoon, and that was the last that we talked for a time.

I left the Navy in the summer of 1976, after receiving an honourable discharge, and temporarily moved in with my mother.

CHAPTER 3

MY CAR

While I was in the Navy, my father co-signed a loan for me to buy a car that a close high school friend had built for himself; it was a dark brown, four-door 1968 Dodge Fury III. He had replaced the original 318 engine with a rebuilt 383 magnum and added a few nice touches like a cam and four-barrel Holley carburetor. To make it a little snappier, he added 390 gears in the rear end. I was impressed on how it looked; at first glance it looked like an old man's car, but with 16-inch tires on the rear and 10-inch on the front and standard deep-walled black rims, it was a beauty to drive and pretty quick when it needed to be. My high school friend said that it could do high 14 seconds in the quarter mile, which for its age and size was pretty good for its day. It had a custom interior, equipped with black high back GTO bucket seats and a wall of gauges.

Now unemployed, I did however have my pension money from the Navy, but knew that it would not last me long. I needed to find work, but had no idea of what I was going to do. Cooking was an option, but it really did not pay that much, and it was not something that I really wanted to do at the time.

MY CRIME SPREE

I attended a party one evening at a high school friend's home and ran into one of the guys who use to hang out with us in school on occasion. Most of my friends didn't like him much, but he always had a wallet full of cash, and never seemed to work. We talked about this and that, and he asked me, "What are you doing for work?"

"Since I got out of the Navy, I really have no idea of what I'm going to do, but I'm going to have to do something soon, as I'm getting short of funds."

He told me we could make some cash together, but we would talk about it one day over a few beers, his treat. So, a few days later we got together at one of the local pubs, and he told me what he thought would be a good way to make a little cash.

The idea was to break into gas stations. He had been doing it alone for some time, but needed someone to be a driver and keep an eye out while he was doing his thing. He went on to say that most garages have a large selection of tools and every garage has a cigarette machine. So, the next afternoon we drove around and staked out a few gas stations outside our local area. We waited until everyone working had gone home. The plan was simple, I would drop him off half a block away, and then find a place to park where I could observe as much of the gas station as I could. He would break in and then find what tools there were to steal, and then hit the cigarette machine, remove and bag up all the cigarettes and coin, and then signal me from the front door. I would pull up behind the gas station and we would load up and be gone.

Together we must have hit about 20 gas stations over a three- to four-month period, we had a great system, which was working well for us, and our pockets were always full of money.

The plan in place was to sell the cigarettes to my connections in the Navy and hit a few gas stations along the way, but first we would drop off the unmarked tools at Jim's, as he had a guy who would sell them for 1/3 of the profit at a local flea market. We then headed for the ferry to Victoria. While on board the ferry, we would stay in my car and roll the change that we got from the cigarette machines and separate the cigarettes by brand in black garbage bags. Once we landed, we would stop at banks along the way to my ex-Navy base, and cash in only a few hundred dollars at a time, as to not raise any suspension with the bank authorities.

When we were got close to the Navy base, I would make a few calls to some of the guys with whom I'd worked on the base and ship. We would then meet at one of the local pubs, where they would purchase the cigarettes from us for half the going rate. The nationwide average price for a pack of cigarettes was about 80 cents, so even selling them for half the price made us some pretty good coin over the next few months.

One day, I was driving to a friend's after getting back from a Victoria run. I had a box of tools in the truck that needed to be disposed of as they were marked with the initials of the previous owner. The box itself was of high quality, not something some 21-year-old would have in his possession. I pulled up to a stop sign and did your typical slow creep though the intersection without stopping.

And just as I got through it, I noticed a police car was coming the other way and just as we passed, he pulled U-turn, turned on his lights, and pulled up behind me. As he exited his car, he said loud and clear, "Turn off your vehicle and keep your hands on the steering wheel."

The first words out of my mouth were "Oh shit." I immediately obeyed as he approached my window and said, "Driver's licence and registration, please." I fumbled around for a bit, and produced the documents he requested.

He then asked me to step out of the car and bring my keys, which I did. We proceeded to the back of my car, and he asked me to open the trunk. I thought, *Oh crap*, and remembered the tools. I opened the trunk and he immediately noticed the toolbox. He opened it up, and pulled out a couple of wrenches, looking at it them closely. That's when he noticed that there were the initials B.C. stamped into all of them. He turned to me, and said, "Well, these look a little expensive for someone of your calibre, not to mention the initials are not the same as yours."

I said, "Yes, sir. I know. They actually belong to a friend of mine."

He said, "Is that right? What's your friend's name?"

"Bill Camp."

He looked at me and smiled. "Well, you stay right here and don't move; I will be right back." He returned to his PC (police car) and proceeded to radio in.

I was now starting to sweat; my heart was starting to pound in my chest, and I was thinking something dumb, like making a run for it, but thought that would be just totally stupid.

He was gone for what seemed a very long time, when he finally stepped out of his car, with my papers in hand. He came up next to me and said, "You know, I know these tools are hot. We've had a rash of break and enters of gas stations in the Lower Mainland, but it would appear that this is your lucky day, as they were not on the hot list of stolen equipment." So, he handed me my licence and registration, and said "You're free to go."

I think I was holding my breath the whole time. I took the papers from him, trying not to shake, and turned around and got back into my car. I took a deep breath, and then realized that I was actually shaking. I started my car and tried to maintain my composure as I pulled out into traffic.

I drove home and pulled into the driveway, put my car in park, and just slumped down into my car seat. My legs refused to move for a moment. That was the last day that I ever did anything like that again. I knew I was God damned lucky, and realized that this was a sign: my days of crime had just come to an end.

MEN IN BLACK

My mother and Uncle John had been separated for about six months. My mom was staying in the house, while Uncle John was staying in Vancouver. My mother had recently spent a week in Kelowna where she met a guy by the name of Larry. Larry was not your typical kind of guy—15 years my mother's junior, which I really didn't like, not to mention, I really did not get a good feeling off him. He was about six feet, tanned, blonde, blue-eyed, and in great physical shape. He drove a custom white Chevy van, and he had built a wooden deck on the top. He would cruise the beaches of Kelowna until he found a place where the parties were happening and then position himself on his deck in his lawn chair and take in the view.

He was a high steel worker from Edmonton, Alberta, and now he was staying with my mom. I had blown a bearing in the rear axle of my car, and I was in the middle of pulling it out when a large black limo pulled into the driveway and parked one car away from mine. The driver got out of the vehicle and proceeded to open the back door. Well, to my surprise, Uncle John stepped out, followed by three rather large men, all dressed in black suits and red silk ties.

It was like a scene out of a gangster movie. I just stood there, taking in everything that I was seeing. My first thought, though, that came to mind was, *Oh, Larry, is about to get a shit kicking or worse.*

Uncle John started walking towards me smiling. I couldn't help but like him. He was always nice to Cindy and I and I have to say he did look after my mother; she never went without when she was married to him. Uncle John had an air of authority about him; chubby as he was, I sensed there was a side to him that I never wanted to see. Looking at me, he said, "What the hell are you doing?"

"I'm working on fixing my car. What's with the men in black?"

He had a deep inner laugh that made me smile. He looked right into my eyes and said, "Johnny, do you trust me?"

I said, "Yes, of course I do."

"Nothing is going to happen to your mother or her boyfriend. I just need you to stay here and not move till I come back, okay?"

Hell, what was I going to do? It was like being caught in a time warp, and all I could do was just nodded my head up and down.

"Good boy. Don't move. I'll be right back." He turned and nodded to the three guys standing next to the limo, and then motioned his head in the direction of the front door. They followed behind him. As Uncle John reached the front door, he reached out and grabbed the doorknob, and just walked right in.

I stood there, looking down at the axle that I just pulled out of my car, and noticed a nice stack of metal shavings. I stood there for a few seconds, looked over at Larry's van parked in front of the house, and then thought, *Oh, what the hell?* I reached down, picked up some of the shavings, and proceeded over to his nice shiny white van. I opened the hood, pulled out the transmission dipstick, put the shavings into the opening, flushed them down with a little engine oil, and replaced the dipstick, closed the hood, and went back to working on my car.

I wasn't sure what was going to happen next at that point. It seemed like an hour hand gone by, but it was only minutes in reality.

The next thing I knew, the four of them came walking out the front door. The three men in black climbed back into the limo and Uncle John walked over to me, reached in his pocket, and said, "Never get your hands dirty if you don't have to." He pulled a small roll of bills from his pocket, peeled off five one-hundred-dollar bills, and handed them to me. As I reached out to take the money, he put his hand on my shoulder and said, "If you ever need anything—anything at all, no matter how big or small—you call the office, day or night, and I mean it, okay?"

Still in a state of shock, I just nodded my head up and down like one of those dog ornaments you used to see in the back window of cars whose heads bob up and down with the motion of the vehicle.

With that said, he turned and walked straight back to the limo, where a man was holding the door open for him. He turned and smiled and waved as he climbed into the back. Then they were gone.

I stood there for moment thinking, *Should I go in the house?* Not knowing what to expect, I was thinking about that my mother, who came out the front door and walked over to me. "Did Johnny talk to you?"

"Yes."

She went on to say, "Everything is okay."

"I know," I said. "Uncle John said everything would be fine."

"I will explain it all to you later," she said.

I said, "Fine," and then proceeded into the house to call a garage to pick up my car and get it fixed.

What it was all about was a little confusing to me at first. But, as it turned out, the whole thing was staged, Uncle John wanted a divorce from my mother, and he also wanted the proceeds of the sale of the house. He wanted grounds for divorce, so he needed to prove that my mother was unfaithful. So, thus, the three men in black were actually witnesses. When Uncle John entered the house, they all proceeded upstairs to the bedroom where they found my mother dressed only in a bath robe, and Larry only in a pair of jeans. The whole thing was staged. In the end Uncle John got his wish, and a few months later my mother and Larry moved to Edmonton, Alberta

After Uncle John's visit, my later mother informed me that I needed to find a place to move to. So, the next day I walked down to the garage to pick up my car, and then headed over to visit my high school friend, Daryl. As I was driving over to Daryl's, I noticed Larry's van was off the side of the road, the hood was up, but he was nowhere to be seen, I smiled to myself and just drove right on by. I found out later from my mother that Larry knew it was me who caused his transmission to seize up.

I arrived at Daryl's and we were sitting around the kitchen table when I mentioned that I was going to have to find a place to live. His mom had overheard us taking and mentioned that they had a fold-out couch in the basement that I was more than welcome to. Daryl was living with his parents and his two younger sisters; they were a great family and took me in without hesitation. For nine months, they made me feel like one of the family.

STREET RACING

One of my biggest thrills was street racing, and I loved the high that I got from it. driving fast can get addictive, and it did for me. I would race anyone who challenged me, and street racing was a huge fad back in the day. This applied to most of my male friends as well; we would spend countless hours just cursing around our local community, checking out where everyone from school was hanging out, and who wanted to race.

OUR FAVOURITE GAME

We had this game we liked to play with the RCMP. We would all get into one car and cruise around until we spotted a police car. We would then drive by slowly in the opposite direction, and when the officer or officers looked our way, we would speed off as fast as we could, as if we had something to hide. This, of course, would almost always get a response from them, and they would immediately turn on their lights and sirens and come after us. We would do our best not to speed, but would do anything within our ability to avoid them, like pulling into a shopping mall, etc.

When they finally caught up to us and pulled us over, they would of course ask all of us to get out of the car. The bravest one of us would wait until everyone had vacated the vehicle, and then lock all the doors from in inside and refuse to come out. The game basically was to see what the officers would do. Most of them would yell and get frustrated, but we knew not to push it too far, and would usually just have fun with the idea of getting them frustrated. It was actually just a prank, but it ended one evening when an officer pulled out his service revolver and tapped it on the window at one of us in the vehicle. We thought it best from then on not to push our luck with this anymore and moved on to something else.

LIGHT THEM UP

One afternoon, a couple of friends and I were cruising around in my car when we saw a couple of girls that we knew from high school walking along the side of the road. They recognized my car and wave at us over, so we pulled over to chat with them. In the midst of the conversation, one of them suggested that we should pick some beer and go hang out some place. We looked at each other and said, "Sure, let's go." So they climbed into the back of my car and we headed off to find the nearest liquor store.

With a case of beer in the car, we were off. I pulled up to the intersection and was waiting for the light to change so I could make a right-hand turn up the hill. The light changed green, and one of my friends said, "Light 'em up."

Well I did just that, the back tires broke free and started to squeal and smoke. By the time I turned the corner, I had filled the intersection with a cloud smoke and could hardly see out my front window, as the inside of the car had also filled up with smoke. As I shot up the hill, I noticed a police car sitting in the downhill line up. He was stuck in the traffic, and I thought, *By the time he gets free, I'll be long gone.* I headed up the hill as fast as I could, then decided to hang a right, and another left and then started too slow down, thinking that I lost him. I hung another left and was feeling a little cocky, when right in front of us were two police cars with their lights on, blocking the road.

I noticed two officers standing behind their cars, with shotguns in their hands, and I came to an immediate stop. Then an officer behind them, whom I did not see at first, proceeded to step forward, and the three of us guys said at the same time, "Oh shit." There in front of us was the father of one of my best friends in the car, Bob. And to top it off, Bob's dad was the staff sergeant of the local RCMP detachment. We knew we were in serious trouble now.

Bob's dad walked up to car and said, "Everyone out." We all got out of the car, and he ordered everyone to the back of my car. He looked into the back seat and spotted the case of beer, then looked at the girls and asked them each for their ID. I actually had no idea that they were underage. Then he looked at me and said, "You do know, of course, you can be charged with supplying alcohol to a minor?"

"Yes, sir."

"And that little stunt that you just pulled at the intersection was not smart. Do you honestly think you can outrun the radio?"

Of course, I'd never thought of that, but I kept my thoughts to myself.

"Well, Johnny, what are we going to do with you?" He then looked over at Bob, and said, "I'll deal with you when I get home tonight." He then took the case of beer out of the back seat of my car and walked up to one of the other officers and said, "Ticket him for dangerous driving, and then let them go." He looked over his shoulder at me and said, "Next time you pull another stunt like that, Johnny, I will put your ass in jail and throw away the key." And I believed him without a doubt.

MY RACING DAYS COME TO AN END

One night, three of my best friends from school—Daryl, Tim, and Ed—and myself were out having a few beers at Tim's, from whom I'd originally bought my car. Ed was helping him tune up his car as Tim had just put together another car, a Chevy Nova. He'd just finished installing a new 350 motor with all the bells and whistles. Tim had been bragging to all of us that it was faster than mine. So we all decided to go for a cruise into Vancouver and go check out the working-class ladies for something to do.

We landed up on the downtown east end by the Bayshore Inn hotel. We both pulled up to the lights side by side. When he started to rev up his engine, I looked over at him and smiled. Daryl said, "Give him a run for his money." The light changed green and I put the gas pedal to the floor, the back tires broke free and started to spin, and smoke started to fill the inside of the car from the burning rubber.

I looked to my right through the passenger window to see where Tim was, and couldn't see him beside me. Looking in my rear-view mirror, I could see that he had backed off. Then when I looked forward again, I could see why. A street washer had just gone by earlier, and the road was wet. The back end of my car started to sway back and forth, and at one point jumped over the curb on the right side of the road. At that point, I hit a telephone pole. With the gas pedal still to the floor and bouncing off the telephone pole, my car then shot across the road, heading into oncoming traffic. I cranked the wheel in the opposite directing, and started heading towards the hotel. I hit the brakes as hard as I could, but we skidded over the curb, and the car went between a telephone pole and light pole, and then down an embankment. I finally got it stopped at the bottom in the hotel public parking lot.

The first thing that I realized was that I had lost my glasses when we went over the embankment. I looked over at Daryl and asked him if he was okay, and his response was, "I think so." We both stepped out of the car, a little shaken, to see what damage was done. The back bumper was sticking up in the air and I had caved in the passenger back quarter panel when I hit the telephone pole. So we got back in the car, started it up and headed to the parking lot exit and headed back home.

We arrived at home no worse for wear, parked my car out front of Daryl's house and went inside to have a few beers after that event.

Tim and Ed, came by a short time later, as they did not see us leave. After we'd gone over the bank, they heard sirens and then the police, fire, and ambulance showed up, so they figured we were on our way home. We were just damned lucky that we hadn't hurt anyone. My car was now beyond repair, so after a few beers, we called it a night and decided to go to bed.

The next morning, Daryl's dad came into my room and said, in a stern voice, "You'd better get up and get dressed. The police are here, and they want to talk to you."

My stomach started to turn over. I got out of bed, got dressed, and went to the front door, where I was met by an RCMP officer.

"Are you John Williams?"

"Yes," I said.

"Is that your car?"

I looked behind him to see that my car was at the time being hooked up to a tow truck. I stated, "Yes, that is my car."

"Come with me," he said.

I followed him down the stairs to the police car, and he opened the passenger door and said, "Have a seat, Mr. Williams." He questioned me about what happened the night before. I told him that the gas pedal got stuck to the floor, I lost control of the car, and we landed up in the parking lot of the Bayshore Inn hotel. And my reason for not sticking around was that the only damage was to my car, so we headed home.

He obviously did not believe me, and he wanted to get a statement from Daryl, who was at the time sleeping soundly in his bed.

So we both walked back to the house. The officer stood in the doorway, while I went downstairs to Daryl's room to wake him up. Once in his room, I turned on his ghetto blaster on low volume, and proceeded to tell him exactly what I had said in my statement. Daryl then got dressed, met the officer at the door, and told him pretty much the same story that I had.

I received six points for dangerous driving, and a fine. Plus, I had to pay for the tow bill, and numerous other bills. I got off easy, and my car was a write-off.

Looking back at it now, we were so lucky that we never really hurt anyone with our wild adventures, never mind any one of us getting seriously hurt or injured for life. Like they say, "Young and Dumb" is the only thing that comes to mind.

So my street racing days came to an end, and I started to think that maybe I had an angel sitting on my shoulder.

I got 36 points on my licence within three months, and was suspended for driving for three months.

With no car, I had to rely on the public bus system. I found out that with my military background, it was actually easy for me to find work in various private security companies. During the next six months, I worked as a security officer in and out of the Vancouver area.

VANCOUVER GENERAL HOSPITAL SECURITY

One of my most memorable experiences was when I was working for a well-known security company that was subcontracted to Vancouver General Hospital. Looking back at my experiences during my time at VGH, I believe that it was a steppingstone to condition me for what was yet to come. I was partnered up with a female officer; we were at the time working the day shift on the weekend. We received a call over our radio that a patient had escaped from the hospital's psychiatric department.

The patient had apparently got past the security door in the 5 D ward; this was the ward where the hospital provided care for patients who suffered from mental disorders. We received a call from one of the parking attendants, saying that he saw a young woman wearing a flowing white night gown running through one of the hospital public parking lots. I was making my rounds at the time, and immediately called in and said I was on my way.

I arrived to find, as described, a woman a little younger than me running between the parked cars in no particular direction. I caught up with her and asked her if she was alright. All of a sudden, she started screaming like a little child having a temper tantrum. I was not trained in how to deal with emotionally disturbed people, so I did my best to try to calm her down, but she did not get much better, so I did the first thing that popped in to my head: I reached out and grabbed her by the arm. When she started resisting, I just flung her up over my shoulder and proceeded back to return her to her ward, kicking and screaming all the way. When I arrived at her ward, the head nurse at the time just looked at me as I approached the desk with this woman over my shoulder, who was now thankfully as quite as a mouse. The head nurse said, "Oh, hell, that works."

THE JUMPER

One sunny day, my partner and I were wandering around the hospital, doing our rounds, when we received a call to report to the emergency department.

When we arrived, the head nurse said that they had just received a patient, brought in by the Vancouver Police. He was in a padded cell and was now banging his head on the door. I was needed to help subdue him. He had been brought in after attempting to jump off the Lions Gate Bridge. He was a big man, of Eastern descent, and from what I could understand from one of the interns, his boyfriend had just broken up with him. I could hear him banging his head on the door, and although it was padded, he could still do himself harm. There were two other interns outside his room at the time, and one of them instructed me to take off my tie and jacket, as we had to go in and restrain him so he could be given a shot to calm him down.

The head nurse of the ward unlocked the door, and the three of us rushed in. He was now standing in the middle of the room totally naked and ready for what was to come next. He then charged forward and took a swing at the first intern, but was unsuccessful, as the second intern shoulder tackled him face down on the floor. I helped hold him down by putting my knee on the back of his shoulders, but he stated kicking and bucking violently. A nurse equipped with a syringe came into the room to inject him and there were legs and arms flaying everywhere. The first naked leg she saw, she stabbed it with the needle. I was totally amazed how strong he was. He was eventually able to get out of our hold on him and stand up. One of the interns stood and then fell to the floor; obviously, he was the one who got the shot.

The next thing we knew, the patient bolted out the door and ran though the emergency waiting room, naked as a jay bird, with my partner and I hot on his heels.

He ran around the corner of the hospital, and went right onto Oak Street; my partner was gaining on him and was about an arm's length way when he saw her and pushed her into some bushes along the sidewalk. I was right behind her and stopped to check if she was okay, and then carried on running after him.

I finally caught up with him in the middle of the Oak Street and West Broadway intersection. I got around him and had him trapped between a bus and a large truck. Traffic had slowed down to a crawl and everyone was taking in the sight of this big naked man in the middle of the road. As I started to talk to him, I could see his eyes rolling in the back of his head. It was a little overwhelming. he started to say he wanted to talk to God, and that he needed His help, so I played along, and told him if he came back with me to the hospital, he could see God and get the help that he needed.

Two police cars pulled up to block the intersection. As the officers were heading in my direction, I put my hand up as to indicate them to stop, which they did. I didn't want them to spook him, and I figured I could talk him into going back up to the hospital. Finally, after about ten minutes, I had him convinced to come with me back to the hospital to see God. We walked back up Oak Street, followed by two police cars, and once we reached the hospital, I walked him right through the front doors of the emergency ward. There were a dozen or more people sitting in the waiting room, some with young children. I finally got him back to the padded cell area, where two interns took him by each arm while a nurse gave him a shot and then placed him back in his padded cell.

After all was send in done, the head nurse of the emergency department came up to me and said, "What the hell were you thinking, walking him through emergency naked?"

I just looked at her and said, "Would you rather have me leave him down on the corner of Oak and Broadway and come back and get a blanket?" I just smiled at her, chuckled, and walked away. In the end, my partner suffered some minor scrapes and a blow to her ego, but everyone was okay.

STABBING VICTIM

It was about 20:00 hrs (8 p.m.) when my partner and I received a call to attend the emergency department. My partner (who was female) and I arrived in emergency and were greeted by the head nurse on duty, who informed us that they had just admitted a woman who had been apparently stabbed numerous times in the abdomen and was immediately being rushed to surgery. Minutes after her arrival, a large middle-aged man arrived. The nurse described him as tall and heavy built. He had confronted the nurse and wanted to know the medial condition of the woman had just been admitted. The nurse also mentioned that he appeared to have been drinking.

He had become very verbally abusive towards her, and was getting more and more frustrated with not getting what he wanted. So she told him that he should step outside and she would see what the woman's condition was and get back to him. He stepped outside the emergency doors just as we had arrived. As I turned to look in that direction, the man she had just described was walking back through the doors and headed in our direction. He started yelling about his girlfriend, and how no one was telling him how she was doing. I told him that she had just arrived, and if he would come with me into the phone room, I would see what my partner could find out from the medical staff. He agreed and followed me into the phone room, which about 10-foot by 12-foot space, with a desk with a phone and an old wooden chair.

I stepped to the back of the room, which was not really a good idea now that I think about it, because the only way out of there was past this very large angry man, who was clearly drunk and in an aggressive mood. He became more and more agitated, even as I tried to assure him that his girlfriend was going to be okay. Just as those words left my lips, he picked up the wooden chair and swung it against the wall, shattering it into pieces. Then he turned, opened the door, and stormed out of the room and out the emergency doors.

I followed him outside. He was now an emotional wreck, crying and angry, I kept my distance and tried to talk to him. I asked him what had happened to his girlfriend. He answered "I fucking stabbed her, maybe." And just at that moment a Vancouver Police car pulled up and two officers got out. The man was leaning up against the hospital wall just outside the emergency entrance. One officer tried to talk to him while the other took my statement of what had happened. They then cuffed him and placed him in the back of their police car. I worked at Vancouver General Hospital for about six months, and a year later after I was hired on as a guard at BC Penitentiary, I was eventually summoned into court to give my statement of the events of what happened that evening. This was my first time in a federal court room. I was sworn in as I took the stand and the crown lawyer asked me, "Can you tell us where you were working on November 12, 1976?"

I responded, "The Vancouver General Hospital, where I worked as a security officer."

"Can you tell me what happened around 20:00 hours (8 p.m.) that evening?"

I proceed to repeat the events that happened.

He then thanked me, and said, "What is it that you do now for a living, Mr. Williams?" I told him that I was a guard at BC Penitentiary. He then smiled and looked at the judge and said, "No more questions, Your Honour." What I found interesting was the defence lawyer did not have any questions for me. The crown council later informed me that the man received five years for assault causing bodily harm.

CHAPTER 4

HEADED IN THE RIGHT DIRECTION

In the spring of 1977, I was attending a close friend's house party. I noticed this very cute woman standing in the corner of the room talking to a group of my friends. I couldn't stop staring at her for some reason; I was captured by her bubbly personality and the way she laughed. When our eyes met, I thought I was going to melt. I found out later that her name was Leslie. Leslie and I hit it right off. I was overcome by her personality and ability to laugh at just about anything. We talked about this and that, and eventually I asked her out on a date. She said that I would have to first meet her parents, and I said okay. She then informed me that her father was a sergeant with the West Vancouver police department. So we hung out the remainder of the evening. I walked her to her car, and we arranged to see one another the next day.

I called her the next day, to confirm, and said that I would pick her up around 7ish. I arrived on time, parked the car in the driveway, and proceeded up to the house. I was a little nervous; I took a deep breath and rang the doorbell. I was relieved that Leslie answered the door. I stepped inside, and removed my shoes. Leslie leaned over and kissed me on the cheek and said, "Don't worry, everything will be fine." She took me by the hand and escorted me down a flight of stairs and through a door at the bottom of the staircase. We entered what appeared to be their TV room.

I noticed her parents curled up on the couch together like two teenagers. Her father immediately got to his feet, stepped forward, and stuck out his hand. I was relieved to see how friendly he was, he was a large, stocky man, and the smile on his face made me feel somewhat relieved. "So you must be John. It's very nice to meet you." Turning, he introduced his wife Gloria, a lovely lady with a bubbly personality. I could see where Leslie got it from. Gloria always gave me a hug and had a friendly smile on her face. I would come to adore her.

Leslie and I dated for about a month or so, I was invited for dinner one evening. As we were sitting around the table, Mr. Ross said, "John, if you're going to continue dating my daughter, you'll need to find a job." He went on to say that he'd heard they were hiring guards at the British Columbia Penitentiary, and with my military background, along with a letter of recommendation from him, he was sure that I would get hired.

The car that I had at the time, an older Dodge Sport, had transmission problems and was in the shop; the bill was $500. I was a little stressed out and went to my father, but he refused to lend me the $500 to have it fixed. I mentioned this at the table. Mr. Ross looked at me and said, "Well, John, I will lend you the money to get your car fixed, and you can pay me back when you can."

Leslie and I broke up some weeks later. I was heartbroken, and they knew it, so they took me up to their cabin in 100 Mile House for a weekend. Mr. Ross was an avid hunter and took me out to teach me what it was all about. He was instrumental in me getting my hunting licence, and when I shot my first moose, he was the first person that I called. I remained in contact with Mr. and Mrs. Ross on and off over the years. On the anniversary of him lending me money to fix my care, I walked up to his front door and handed him an envelope containing five one-hundred-dollar bills.

PENITENTIARY SERVICE OF CANADA

In early April 1977, I went to the New Westminster employment office and applied to the employment posting. Two days later I received a phone call to report to the old warden's residence on the BC Penitentiary property where the interviews will be conducted at 0900.

On the day of my interview, I showed up wearing a three-piece suit, sporting a military-style haircut, and a leather briefcase in hand, still having that walking tall and military aura about me.

British Columbia Penitentiary

I remember entering the waiting room, looking around and seeing about half a dozen other guys, who looked like they had just finished working for a construction site—dressed in jeans and some in work boots sitting or slumped in various sitting positions around the room. I felt a little tad uncomfortable, as I looked as if I was dressed for a business meeting.

This tall slim striking gentleman in uniform entered the room, took a look around the room and pointed his finger at me, and said, "You're next. Come with me." I got up smartly and followed him through the door into what appeared to be his office. He pointed to a chair in front of the desk and said, "Take a seat, son." I placed my briefcase on the floor and sat down in the chair.

He sat behind the disk, looking over some papers, which I assumed to be my employment application. He looked up over his glasses at me and said, "So I see you served in the Canadian Armed Forces."

I replied, "Yes, sir, I did."

"It also looks like you come highly recommended by a Mr. Jack Ross of the West Vancouver police department."

I answered again, "Yes, sir."

He looked at me, said, "I am going to ask you some questions," and then proceeded to pull out a note pad and pen. "So here is the first question. You are a guard, and you are assigned to take a work party of five inmates outside the front gate to sweep and clean around the area. Some time goes by, and you notice that one of your inmates has disappeared. What would you do?"

Just as I was about to respond, he said, "You would, of course, radio in and let someone know what has happened, and then return back to inside with the rest of your work party. Yes?"

I just looked at him and said, "Yes, sir."

The next question he asked was, "If you were on tower duty, and you saw an inmate going over the wall, would you shoot to kill or shoot to wound?"

This time he did not answer the question for me, so I took a few minutes to think about it. "I would shoot to wound, sir."

He then responded, "Yes, that is a good answer."

We went through a few more series of questions about dealing with security issues, and then he said, "Well, I think that is all that I need for now." He stood from his chair, extended his hand, and said, "Congratulations. Someone will contact you as to when to report for work."

The next day, I received a phone call informing me that I had to report to the front gate of the BC Penitentiary the following day at 0800.

I arrived the next day right on time and was greeted at the front gate by an older gentleman in uniform. I said that I was told to report to the front gate.

"Ah, yes," he said. "So you're one of the Tree's new recruits." I found out later that "the Tree" was the nickname of the officer who had interviewed me. The older gentleman introduced himself as Ralph and he was dressed in what appeared to be a uniform that was in dire need of ironing; he wore no tie, had an open collar, and no forge cap. I was a little puzzled, being still pretty fresh out of the military dress where deportment was always a priority. He had at least a two days' growth on his face, but he was friendly enough, and escorted me into the front gate to an office just inside, where there were three other guys sitting, who I assumed were also new.

About 15 minutes later, Mr. George Elms, the officer who hired me, arrived dressed in his CX 6 uniform, I really didn't notice how tall he was, and chuckled to myself when I thought about how he got his nickname.

We walked through the inner gate and once outside, we proceeded up a large set of stairs up a hill towards the upper level of the prison. Looking up, I could see what appeared to be one of the main cell blocks. It was a very large building, with bars all over the windows. The interior of the main courtyard was beautifully landscaped, with flowers and small mixed bushes along the walkway.

Inner courtyard BC Pen

We entered a building and lined up along a long counter, where we filled out a piece of paper that give them our sizes of clothing, shoes etc. We tried on the uniform, which more looked like that a bus driver would wear. Then we were taken to what was called the main hall; it was the main entrance leading into the cell block area and also housed the radio room and various offices, as well as the inmate court room, and below was the officers lounge. We were to begin getting briefed on security measures and would be given a tour of the inside of the institution. The whole event took about four hours, and then Mr. Elms handed us a piece of paper and told us to report to the main hall for on-the-job training at 0700 hrs the next day.

DAY ONE

As instructed, I reported to the main hall the next day, and reported to the keeper's office. There were two classifications of guards at the time, correctional and security. Security worked mostly armed posts, towers, and gun walks, and actually had little to no contact with the inmate population. Seeing that I wanted to work indoors, I was assigned to the correctional sector. Back when I started, there was no real prior training; there was, however, a few days of orientation training. I worked for six months before I actually got any training. I contributed this to the simple fact that the institution was seriously suffering from staff shortages. I was assigned to work with a crew of seasoned guards in the north wing; I was 21 years old at the time.

I remember the long walk up from the front gate to the main hall every day, thinking, *What a lot of stairs just to get to work.* We mustered in what was known as the main hall. We lined up against a long wall much like in the military, and the CX 6, who was the supervisor on day shift and cleverly nicknamed "the keeper," would take role call and inspect the dress and deportment of the officers coming on shift.

Seeing that I was relatively still fresh out of the military, my uniform was freshly ironed, there were creases down the front of my pants, and my boots where spit shined—you could almost count your teeth in them. I looked up and down the line, to see my fellow officer dressed mostly in well-worn pants and uniform jackets, and boots that had not seen polish in some time. The day shift keeper noted my dress and said, "Do you all see this young officer? Every one of you should take his example of how an officer should look." I of course wore numerous negative comments from my fellow senior officers, who said, "You just wait. You'll look like the rest of us in time. Fortunately, that never happened; it was too engrained in me to not respect the uniform, which had been drilled into me in my military basic training.

NICKNAME

It was traditional that working at BC Pen, guards never used their real names; this was a way to protect our identity. I was first nicknamed Willy, due to my last name being Williams, but shortly thereafter we had a new officer assigned to our crew, and he insisted that he be called Willy. So one of my fellow officers said, "So, what did you do in the Navy?" I responded I was a cook on a destroyer, so for the next 36 years, I came to be known as "Cookie." Even to this day, and after years of being retired, still many of my associates and friends still call me by my nickname.

The north wing was a cold and drafty place to work at the best of times; the main dome had several broken windows facing the west side of the dome area, which reached up to the gun walk, five tiers high (five storeys high). The weather and wind, along with various types of birds, flew in and out of the main dome area, leaving inches thick residue behind on the bars. It amazed me that they were never replaced the windows until the day they announced that the BC Penitentiary was going to close. I am sure it would not been as impressive for those thousands of people who toured the 102-year-old prison.

HIGH FIVES

I remember one of my first assignments once I had completed the basic induction course, on how to open cells, which consisted of two wheels that looked like something you would see on an old sailing ship. Cells could be opened individually as well as all opened all at once. But you always had to check the wheels on the beginning of your shift, as I was warned by a few fellow senior officers that inmates would on occasion tape half-broken razor blades to the fingers of the wheels. In the years that I worked there, I never came across this. At the time, the north wing housed only 60 inmates; this was due to the riot that took place on September 27, 1976. It was the largest riot in the history of the BC Penitentiary; it lasted six days, and ended peacefully on October 2, 1976.

After the riot, they closed ¾ of the east wing cell block, due to the amount of damage done during the riot. It originally held 260 inmates, but it now it only held 52, and the north wing at the time held 99 inmates.

I was working day shifts alone on what was known as the high fives, which is the top tier in the north wing of BC Pen.

Back in the day it was pretty simple. There were three things in the inmate's daily routine: work, yard, or lock up. The BC Penitentiary did not have a dining room for the inmates, so the inmates had to eat their meals in their cells. The day shift keeper would be on the floor of the dome and would be responsible for the daily security and routine of the wing assigned to him.

He would yell out his commands, such as "open them up," in which case we would open all the cells on our tier so they could go down and pick up their dinner tray. The keeper on the floor would usually call for two tiers at a time so as not to have a large number of inmates all out at once. On occasion, depending on who the keeper on at the time was, he might call for the whole north or east wing to be released. The inmates would then proceed to the kitchen to pick up their meal trays and proceed back to their cells to eat and be locked up.

East wing tier wheel

North wing

North wing office

While working the on Tier 5, one of my responsibilities was to supervise the inmate cleaner on my tier; I was told that the cleaner on my tier was a 2x lifer, a well-seasoned inmate and a long-time resident.

I remember one day we had just let the inmates out to return their food trays to the kitchen and proceed to work, or the yard, or be locked up in their cells. As soon as they had left, we would walk down each tier to ensure that every cell was secured. One particular morning, as I was walking down the 5C tier, there were a few stragglers on the range. I walked past them in their cells, and proceeded to the end of the tier when one of them stepped out from his cell and started to tease me about being such a young bull, a common phrase for a new guard.

This seasoned inmate wanted to know if I wanted to have a cigarette, and to join him in his cell. This of course made me feel really uncomfortable, being so new. Not sure how to respond to what he said, I proceeded back down the range to lock him in. I heard someone clearing his throat behind me. The inmate looked past me, and then quietly stepped into his cell as I locked him up. I turned to exit the tier, and saw the cleaner was leaning on his mop. He looked at me as I approached and said, "Let me give you some advice there, young fella. There are three basic rules that you should know when dealing with the likes of us, first of all, respect is a two-way street, and inmates in here understand two things, yes and no. There is no maybe. Always look us in the eyes and stand your ground, and never back up when confronted, because if you do, they will never have any respect for you." I spent a week working on the high fives, and never forgot his advice my whole career.

During my time at BC Penitentiary, it was a whole new life-learning experience. I enjoyed the comradeship with my fellow officers, who came from all walks of life—some not as young as me, but many were in their mid to mature ages with years of experience. I learned, during my short time in the Armed Forces, to pick the brain of those who have experience.

I saw and experienced much in my three years at BC Pen. They say you have never truly experienced what jail is all about until you walk the tiers alone. And whoever said that was right on the money.

Typical cell

I was working in the north wing one afternoon shift, and being the new rookie, we always got the duties that the senior officers never liked to do. This one afternoon shift, a gentleman from visits came up to the main dome to hand out the inmate mail. Back in those days, the mail was actually delivered to the inmates in their cells after the afternoon count was correct. I remember hearing stories about this gentleman from some of the senior guards.

He was at one time a guard himself back in the early days and was a bit of a shit disturber towards the inmates for years, as I remember it. Then one day he received a package at his home, as it turned out, it was a bomb. As a result, he lost both his hands in the blast, and as a result, he was fitted with two prosthetic hooks, that enabled him to pinch and grasp items.

We headed down the east wing, where he started to hand out the mail and put it on the bars of the inmate's cell. There were a couple of inmates that made comments, those that did, he refused to put their mail on the bars, but instead held on to the letters with one clasp, and when the inmate went to reach for it, he would try and snap the inmate with the other claw. Of course, the inmates would swear and curse him, but he would just laugh. It was not something that I expected, and I was taken fully off guard, and really felt uncomfortable walking on the tiers with him. It was no wonder most of the senior guards didn't want to escort him down the ranges.

I watched how some of the more experience senior guards communicated with the inmates, some guards had their favourites, of course, along with those inmates who I found out later were also their informants.

There were only two kinds of population back when I first started in the service; the first one was of course general population, and the second was protective custody. After the riot in 1976, the total population of BC Penitentiary was around 250 inmates, 40-some odd of which were protective custody, housed under the B-7 wing, segregated from the general population inmates.

There were three major areas that held prisoners when I started at BC Penitentiary: the north wing, the east wing, and on the eastern side of BC Pen was B-7 upper and lower, and the punitive and segregation unit (SMSU), or the "penthouse," as many came to call it. It was located on the top of B-7 and housed a mixture of population and protective custody inmates.

FIRST HANGING

I remember my very first inmate hanging experience, it was in June 1978, and I was reporting for day shift in the PCU unit; when I arrived on post, the graveyard shift had been relieved and it was policy to do a count when you take over the shift. There were two other officers with me at the time; I remained in the office while the two of them conducted the morning count. They weren't gone very long when one of them came running back to the office and said, "Call the nurse and the keeper. We have a hanger." I made the necessary calls and remained in the office until help arrived.

When the keeper and the nurse arrived, I told them what tier the officers were on; they proceeded to the tier immediately.

Minutes had gone by when one of the officers I was working with returned to the office and said that the inmate was dead, and that the keeper had sent him back to get a stretcher and blanket.

The officers on the morning shift had completed their count an hour before they were relieved, and really didn't notice anything wrong at the time. They said the last time they saw the inmate who hanged himself, he was sitting at the back of his cell and appeared to be okay.

When the day shift count was being conducted, the officers thought the same thing; then, on second glance, they realized that he was actually hanging in a sitting position from a wooden stake in the wall just above his head. He apparently had made a noose out of one of his sheets, and as I was told later, he actually choked himself to death.

He was only 22 years old; we found out later that day, from one of the other inmates on his tier, that he was getting pressured for sexual favours from another inmate who was a high-profile sexual predator. I always wondered why he never mentioned it to anyone or told someone what he was going through; he was not much older than me at that time.

CLIFFORD ROBERT OLSON

During my time working in the protective custody unit of BC Pen, I got to meet the notorious Clifford Olson on more than one occasion.

Clifford Robert Olson was born in 1940 on New Year's Day in Vancouver, British Columbia, he spent most of his life in trouble with the law and in a quarter of a century, he logged some 94 convictions between the years of 1957 to 1981.

Olson was first convicted of burglary in 1957. He was sentenced to nine months in jail, but later escaped, and was picked up soon thereafter. During the course of his incarceration, Olson escaped six times.

While in jail, Olson was known as an informant and an aggressive homosexual. He was very much a manipulator and once coached a fellow inmate, Gary Marcoux, into confessing his recent charges of rape and mutilation and murder of a nine-year-old girl. Olson then landed up being an informant at Marcoux's trial. Olson never did anything without a reason, and that reason usually only benefited his own selfish ego.

Olson was released from jail September 7, 1980; in November 1980 he began his killing spree, Christine Weller a 12-year-old girl was abducted from her home in Surrey, BC. Her body was later found on Christmas Day, only to be followed by another. Thirteen-year-old Colleen Diagnault went missing from her Surrey, BC, home on the 16th of April. Darren Johnsrude, 16 years of age, was abducted from a shopping mall in Vancouver, BC, only later to be found dead on May 2nd.

On May 15th, Olson married his long-time sweet heart and four days later, Sandra Lynn Wolfsteiner, who was 16 years of age, went missing while hitchhiking in Langley, BC. Thirteen-year-old Ada Anita Court went missing on June 21st from Coquitlam, BC.

On the 2nd of July, 9-year-old Simon Patrick James Partington of Surrey, BC, disappeared while riding his bike to a friend's house.

On July 9th 14-year-old Judy Kozma went missing, her body only later to be found near Weaver Lake by Agassiz, BC, on July 25th.

Olson was already a suspect at the time of the disappearances. Police kept a close eye on his movements, but they were unable to prevent him taking another four victims by the end of July. Raymond King, 15 years old, went missing from New Westminster, BC, July 23rd; two weeks later his body was also found on the shores of Weaver Lake, near Agassiz, some two weeks later. Sigrun Arnd 18 years of age went missing on July 25th in Vancouver, BC, while thumbing rides; her remains were identified only by her dental charts. Another victim, Terri Carson, disappeared from Surrey, BC; her body was also recovered from Weaver Lake on July 30th. Louise Chartrand, 17, went missing while hitchhiking in Maple Ridge, BC, and died July 30th.

The police were following Olson and arrested him days later, after he picked up two females who were hitchhiking on Vancouver Island. A search of his vehicle revealed an address book, containing the name of one of his victims, Judy Kozma; he was charged with her murder six days later.

Olson struck a deal with the prosecution on four known victims; he would receive $10 000 per victim and directions to the six outstanding bodies. Olson pled guilty on January 11, 1982, to 11 counts of murder and was sentenced to 11 concurrent life terms.

The Olson case is one for the history books. His long history of crime escalated into one of Canada's most historic criminals. His case raised questions not raised before, but it did eventually help an ongoing movement regarding the rights of victims.

My dealings with Clifford were short and sweet, what I remember about him was that he was always overly friendly with the guards, and he liked to spend more time hanging out around our office and bum coffee from most of the guards who were on duty.

He was not overly bright, but he was a smooth talker and always kept the guards informed on what was going on in the protective custody unit, which labelled him a "rat."

Clifford Olson died on September 30, 2011.

MY FIRST SLASHING

I was assigned to working the graveyard shift in B-7 wing one evening; apparently there had been a brew party that night, with about ten inmates participating. The officers on the previous shift found the leftovers of a homemade brew, which usually consists of bread (yeast) for the ferment stage and fruit and sugar. It's hard to keep the smell from getting out, and it is all about the alcohol, not the taste. Mind you, over the years I have actually tasted some pretty good brews; these are usually made by someone with some experience, who was usually nicknamed "brew master."

Alcohol and drugs are extremely dangerous inside jails. People's personality changes, violence occurs for no apparent reason, and when you have a group of them in this condition, it's a powder keg waiting to explode.

I was the only one working in B-7 on graveyards. All the inmates were locked up, so I grabbed my punch clock, which is a clock-looking device wrapped in leather with a leather strap; and at the end of each range there was a punch station, the officer I relieved said that the nurse had been down after the evening count to deliver medication, but she was refused to deliver medication on that tier due to the fact that most of the inmates had been drinking.

Punch clock

So, with punch clock in hand, off I went to punch the tiers. As I proceeded onto the tier where they had been drinking, I was overcome with the smell of fresh-drunk brew, it reeked heavily in the air. As I reached the end of the tier, an inmate came up to his cell bars, asking me if the nurse was going to come and give him his medication. I could sense the strong aroma of brew on him. I informed him that the nurse was not coming down to deliver meds and stated the reason. I could sense his frustration in his body language to my response and after punching the clock, I turned and headed back off the tier.

I finished my rounds of B-7, and it was pretty quiet for the time being, so I thought it would be a good time to make a coffee and kick back and relax until my next round. A few minutes later, all hell broke loose.

I could hear inmates yelling, "There's is a guy here that's slashed up. He needs to see the nurse right fucking now." So I headed back down the tier to see what was going on. When I reached the cell of the inmate who had asked me about the nurse, I could see he was sitting on the edge of his bed in a T-shirt and undershorts. He had slashed both his forearms with what I suspected was a razor blade. He looked at me and said, "Get me the fucking nurse, right now." I headed back off the tier to my office and called the keeper on duty and let him know what the situation was.

The keeper said that he would call the nurse and let her know, and that he would escort her down as soon as possible. Minutes after I had hung up the phone, the inmates on the tier started yelling and shouting and banging their cell bar doors with their metal coffee mugs. The keeper and nurse arrived a few minutes later. Through all the banging and yelling, she decided that she was not going to go down the tier to see the inmate. So the keeper looked at me and said, "You go down the tier and I will open his cell, and you bring him here to the office."

Well, I was not fond of that idea, as the yelling and banging had now escalated to where the inmates were lighting rolls of toilet paper on fire and throwing them off the tier. So I took a deep breath and worked my way back down the tier to where the inmate was. When I looked into his cell, I could see him slouched over on his side on the bed, unconscious. Not knowing if he passed out from drinking or blood loss, I yelled for the keeper to open his door. Now the cells are not very big, and the beds would fold up against the wall. Unfortunately, I would not be able to do that now.

So when the keeper spun the wheels so that I could unlock his door, the only way I could see me getting him out of there was to drag him out backwards.

I stepped into his cell. As I looked down, I could see that I was standing in a puddle of his blood. I just reached around and manoeuvred him into a sitting position on the bed. Then I turned his back to me and reached under his arms and grasping my hands together across the front of his chest. I lifted him up and started to back out of the cell with his arms draped at his side and blood dripping down his arms as I dragged him backwards down the tier.

Once off the tier, the nurse came and told me to lay him on a stretcher that the keeper had placed on the floor outside the office. His wounds, she said, were superficial, and she pointed out to me that he had done this more than once. I could see scars on both his forearms. She checked his breathing and blood pressure, then reached into her first aid bag and bandaged up his wounds.

He started to regain consciousness and she put him up in a sitting position on the stretcher. She looked at him and said, "That's not a bright thing to do."

He looked down and said, "All I wanted was my medication."

She snarled back, telling him, "You're acting like a child." Then she reached into her bag and pulled out some medication for him for the pain, and told him to come to the morning medication line and she would give him some more. He had calmed down at this point, and was a little more passive. The keeper asked him if he wanted to get a mop and bucket to clean up his cell. He said that he would do it the next day, so I escorted him back to his cell and closed his door. The keeper locked him in for the remainder of the evening.

With the keeper and nurse back on their way to the main hall, I proceeded to make myself another coffee, and put pen to paper, as report writing was something that I was going to have to get used to. The rest of the night went without incident, and I was happy to get home, but tossed and turned thinking about what happened, just one of many slashing's to come.

FIVE STAND

October 5, 1978, I was working day shift. The morning count was correct, and the inmates were either reporting to work or going to the yard. I was assigned to stand five in the exercise yard, it was a nice sunny day and there were approximately 50 inmates in the yard. My stand overlooked the weigh pit area; I was watching inmate Milmind working out on a weight bench. He was adding 50-lb plates to his bench press bar, and I noted that he had approximately 250 lbs on the bar.

He was a quite individual, a dedicated weightlifter who kept to himself mostly, serving his first federal sentence for robbing numerous Brinks armoured trucks back in Ontario; the rumour was the money was never found. He was soon to be released back to Ontario to be with his wife and daughter. I observed inmate Quiring quickly walking over to the weight pit. Quiring was your typical seasoned inmate who had status among the other inmates as being a hard ass, and someone not to confront. He was also an aggressive homosexual, who usually took advantage of the new young inmates that came into the pen. He was about the same size of Milmind, but not nearly in as good of shape as Milmind.

He walked into the weight pit and confronted Milmind. A heated argument soon broke out between them, and the next thing I observed was Quiring attempting to take a swing at Milmind. I was thinking to myself, *This is going to be good.* Milmind stepped back just as Quiring swung. He missed, and then Milmind grabbed Quiring by the throat with one hand and literally lifted him up so he was on his tippy toes, and then slammed Quiring onto the weight bench, and started to punch Quiring around the head. I jumped off my chair, grabbed the shotgun next to me, and yelled at them to break it up. As I said that, I cocked the shotgun, putting a shell into the chamber. The next thing that happened was six inmates ran into the weight pit and surrounded both inmates, so as to protect them, and broke it up. The exercise yard was cleared, and Milmind and Quiring were taken to the hole and charged for fighting.

On court day, Milmind was in lock up in a single cell in the main hall where court was held, waiting to see the judge. I walked by the cell and he said to me, "Hey, boss, you got a minute?" I said sure. He then proceeded to thank me for stopping the fight. He said Quiring had heard that he was going to be to be released and wanted Milmind to do him a few favours on the street. When he refused, Quiring threatened his family. He continued to say if I had not stopped it, he said Quiring might have killed him. He went on to say that he was to be released in about a week, and wanted to know if it was possible to remain in the penthouse (SMSU) until then. He went on to say that he would never come back to prison again. I never did come across him again.

MY INTRODUCTION TO THE NOTORIOUS ANDY BRUCE

Convicted murderer Andy Bruce was sentenced to life in prison in 1970, after a contract killing reportedly commissioned over one ounce of heroin. He shot the young female victim twice, only stopping when his gun jammed. Bruce has always denied being the gunman.

On June 11, 1975, inmates Dwight Lucas, Claire Wilson, and Bruce took 15 hostages, including Mary Steinhauser, a 32-year-old old social worker. It was rumoured she was having an affair with Bruce. An armed squad ended the 41-hour hostage-taking. Mary Steinhauser was killed in the exchange and Bruce was shot twice, once in the head, but survived.

I was working on the lower floor of B-7. My post at that time was to control movement in and out of what we called the back door. It accessed the main compound and led to a road along the east side of the B-7 wing and down the long rolling stairs that led to the front gate. The visit building was located south of the main gate. All inmate movement inside the compound was controlled by a pass system.

Earlier that morning, I had let inmate Martin through as he had a visit. A short time later, officer Roy Yasuda was escorting Andy Bruce from the SHU unit down to the visiting building. We nodded and said hello to one another as I unlocked the steel door and let him and Andy Bruce into the compound.

Bruce at the time was in body restraints and leg irons. Approximately 20 minutes later, there was a ring at the door; I opened it to find inmate Martin standing behind the steel barrier. I noticed that he no longer had on his winter green parka. He appeared agitated and stressed. "Let me in, quick."

I said, "Where is your jacket?"

He just looked at me with panic in his eyes and said, "For fuck's sake, let me in."

Sensing that something was not right, I unlocked the steel barrier door. He immediately shot past me, ran over to the supervisor on duty, and said, "You have a serious problem in visits, Andy Bruce and some others have taken hostages in visits."

The supervisor on duty immediately called central control and reported what he had been told by inmate Martin. Shortly after the call, the institution immediately went on lock down.

VISITORS TAKEN HOSTAGE

There was a total of eight inmates in the screen visiting area of V&C at the time of the incident, five of whom were very high profile: Andy Bruce, serving a life sentence; Stephen Hall, who recently at the time failed an escape attempt; Ralph Saumer, who was in for robbery; and David Bennett, who was serving a 10-year sentence for armed robbery.

The V&C staff were first alarmed when they heard the sound of breaking glass coming from the screen visiting area; somehow, the inmates managed to get themselves a .38 revolver. They attempted to shoot the lock off the door that led from the screened area to the visitors' side of V&C. This was unsuccessful, which enabled the staff to get safely away though the front entrance and to lock the front door of V&C, containing the inmates inside.

Andy Bruce, who was being escorted by Officer Yasuda, was still on the inmate side of the screen visits. Inmate Hall, who was armed with a homemade knife, demanded the keys from Officer Yasuda so they could remove the body restraint belt from Bruce. Officer Yasuda refused to give Hall the keys. Hall then stabbed Officer Yasuda in the neck, and when Officer Yasuda was on the floor, Hall took the keys off him.

Seriously injured, Officer Yasuda managed to get himself out the inmate access door and to the front gate. The officer at the front gate at the time had served as a medic in the army and was able to control Officer's Yasuda's bleeding until a nurse arrived.

Now contained in the V&C area, the inmates had no place to escape. Bruce had been shot in the leg by a ricocheted bullet when they had attempted to shoot the lock off the door. At this point, no one else was injured, including the visitors.

The following day, two visitors were released for exchange of drugs, food, and cigarettes. The institutional doctor refused to allow the inmates to take the drugs themselves, which resulted in them coming out one at a time out the inmate access door to V&C to get their injections.

The following night another hostage was released, again for more Demerol, cigarettes, and food.

On Thursday, February 2, negotiations continued. The hostage-takers were concerned as t0 the condition of Officer Yasuda, and as to what charges they could possibly be facing. More hostages were released during the day, again for more drugs and food; from the back of B-7, we could see smoke coming from the chimney of V&C. Later, we found out that the inmates were burning all the inmate V&C files to stay warm.

Inmates Saumer and Bennett turned themselves over to the RCMP and were taken into custody and placed in lock up in Burnaby. Two more hostages were released before the evening ended.

On Saturday, February 4th, it was all over. The news media swarmed the front gate; they actually reported that the incident was handled well, although there was $70 000 worth of damage to the V&C

HOSTAGE SUSPECTS ACQUITTED
ON ESCAPE PLOT CHARGES

During the hostage-taking of V&C inmate, Andy Bruce's visitor was a one Sandra Meadley; she was the daughter of Betsy Wood, who was a prison activist and had been since my arrival at BC Pen. Steven Hall's visitor was Betsy Wood. David Bennett's visitor was Gay Hoon, who was also an active prison reformer. I had seen Betsy Wood and Gay Hoon hanging around the BC Pen grounds on more than one occasion.

In February 1978, Gay Hoon and Betsy Wood appeared in court, charged with being accomplices in the escape plot. The car that they had arrived in the day of the hostage incident had been traced to Betsy Wood, and when it was searched, men's clothing was found inside. But in the end, charges were withdrawn as the judge decided that the evidence against them mainly was weak, at best.

Later on that year, those inmates who took part in the hostage-taking went to court. Hall received a second life term for his actions against Officer Yasuda. Andy Bruce and David Bennett received sentences that ran concurrently with those that they were serving at the time of the hostage-taking.

There however was one startling piece of evidence that Andy Bruce revealed in the court room. He stated that Officer Pondelicek had agreed to bring in the gun in return for money and drugs. Pondelicek denied the allegations against him. During the trial, the evidence given failed to convince the jury and Pondelicek was acquitted of all charges.

It is not easy going to court, although I have been in court a few times myself over the years. The hardest thing is when your accused of something that you didn't do. Other officers around you start to wonder about your creditability. I knew Officer Pondelicek and had worked with him on many occasions over the years at the BC Penitentiary. I always enjoyed working with him; he was an honourable kind of guy, and what always impressed me about him was that he took pride in his day-to-day work, and his dress and deportment were as good as mine.

After the BC Pen shut down, I lost contact with a good number of officers that I worked with during my three years at the Pen.

OFFICER CHARGED WITH ASSAULT AND CAUSING BODILY HARM

In 1978, an officer was charged with common assault and causing bodily harm on am inmate. The assaults apparently occurred while inmate Miller was in the penthouse (SMSU) in October 1976.

Several inmates testified in court that the officer had thrown hot water on Miller and assaulted him. During the evening routine, it was common to give the inmates hot water in their cells to make a coffee. The officer was accused of having thrown a pail of hot water on Miller. The following day, the rumour was that Miller was removed from his cell and the guard hit him in the face and kicked him in the groin. The inmate was seen by the institutional nurse on duty and she testified in court that there were no visual marks on Miller, other than a slight cut on his chin.

In his defence, the officer said that Miller, who was in handcuffs at the time and was going to the exercise yard, and tried to assault him while passing him and the inmate had to be restrained.

In the end, the officer was acquitted on all charges as the judge stated that the injuries inmate Miller had could have been inflicted by someone else.

WORKMAN'S COMPENSATION WIN

During my three years working in the BC Penitentiary, it received a lot of negativity from the media and the public at large, but efforts were being made to improve the conditions of the 100-year-old prison at the time. And changes were coming; one of those changes was a new open visiting program. Inmates who were in general population and protective custody qualified for this program. They would no longer have to sit across from their visitor separated by a plastic window. They now would now be allowed to sit across a table from the visitor. Visitors who put in for this program would be screened through a process christened the "visits review committee." Of course, they had to sit across from one another, and although holding hands was permitted, kissing or necking was not allowed, and any breach of the rules would terminate their visit.

The open visiting program was a new concept and most of the officers I worked with were not too fond of this new visiting program. More than one officer expressed their concerns, that it would be a new way to bring contraband into the prison.

During my first year working at the BC Penitentiary, officers were encouraged and allowed to use the gym during their lunch hour when the institution was locked down after the noon-hour count. I spent three days a week working out in the gym. One day I accidently broke my wrist; I was working out on the heavy bag with my hands wrapped like a boxer. It was almost getting time to report back to my post. I removed the wraps and my partner Toney, who was holding the bag for me at the time, decided to swing it in my direction. I stepped back and hit it with everything that I had, and then at that very instant I felt a sharp pain shot through my wrist. Toney said, "I think you need to go see the nurse as I think you broke it." So off we went to go see the nurse, with me holding my arm against my chest.

Once we arrived, the nurse looked at me and said, "Well, I do believe that you might have broken it." She then picked up the phone and called the central control and said that I would need to be taken to the hospital for an x-ray. Toney returned to his post, and I was on my way to the hospital, escorted by a fellow officer. We arrived at the Royal Columbian emergency, and being in uniform, I was rushed in to see the attending physician on duty. He took a quick look at my wrist, and said, "First things first. We need to get an x-ray."

As it turned out, I had broken a small bone, called the scaphoid. Apparently, I hit the bag with such force that a muscle came away from the bone, and when it snapped back, it broke the scaphoid bone. So the attending physician set my wrist, put me in a cast, and sent me back to work.

When I returned to the institution, I was instructed to fill out the necessary paperwork before being sent home. So I had to fill out an observation report and Workman's Compensation forms as to what occurred. After this was completed, I was sent home on sick leave, until my Workman's Compensation claim went through.

A week later, I received a call from my keeper, informing me that my claim had been denied. Seeing that I did not have an enough sick leave to carry me through until the cast was removed, I would have to return to work, but would be put on light duties. I would then be assigned to the Visit and Correspondence department, until my cast was removed and I was cleared for active duty.

Upon my return to work a few days later, I contacted our union PSAC (Public Service Alliance of Canada) representative, and was told that I would have to file an appeal. He was not sure that I would win, but it was worth a try. The following week, I drove in to the PSAC regional office in Vancouver, and met the gentleman, Cecil, who would be taking my case. He was an older gentleman, short stocky, and had worked for PSAC for a number of years.

The problem with my claim was that we needed to prove that officers were encouraged to maintain a physical level during their working hours. So, I returned to work and started to ask my fellow officers if there was anything in writing, in regard to working out in the gym. As it turned out, I did find some written documentation. After searching through endless files, I found the minutes of a meeting with the union where management encouraged all staff to use the gym during their lunch hour.

Encouraged by this document, I called my representative, Cecil, and informed it of what I had found. I read it to him over the phone, and he seemed very pleased.

Six weeks later, Cecil and I were to meet with the Workman's Compensation review board to go over my claim. We walked into their board room, and were greeted by three men, who introduced themselves. We all sat down, and Cecil pulled out his files and started to go through the paperwork that I found. He explained that we were encouraged to maintain some level of fitness due to the conditions of our work. This only took about 15 minutes to accomplish, then the board member in charge asked if we could step out of the room until they reviewed the documentation and they would call us back in when they made their decision.

It took about 20 minutes. Cecil and I were called back into the boardroom. We sat down and waited as the chairperson looked up from the files and said, "We have considered all the information presented to us today, and the board members voted unanimously in support of your claim."

As it turned out, we had actually won a huge historic victory for all other departments, such as the police officers and firefighters, who were also encouraged to maintain a physical level of physical fitness during their working day. I later found out that our case was listed in the WCB manual as a win.

APPOINTMENT TO SMSU UNIT

On July 9, 1979, I was assigned to the super max secure unit (SMSU) squad, which many of us had come to call the penthouse; it was located on the upper floor of B-7 wing.

One of the four ranges of the penthouse in the BC Penitentiary, showing the elevated catwalk along which armed guards monitored prisoners' movement and feeding, showering. Any time the officers were on the cell range, they were equipped with a .38 revolver.

I spent about four months in the penthouse. It was a high-security unit that housed approximately 44 inmates.

SMSU exercise yard

The segregation exercise yard was built after the McCann decision to provide prisoners with a daily one-hour open air exercise time.

CRUEL AND UNUSUAL PUNISHMENT CASE

McCann was an inmate in the BC Penitentiary who had spent 1421 days in solitary confinement; he along with six other inmates filed a claim in the Federal Court of Canada, June 4, 1974.

Their claim was based on the fact that conditions on which they lived in were cruel and unusual. When I first reported to the penthouse, as we had come to nickname it, it could best be described as being reminiscent of a dungeon.

The cells were small, approximately 6 feet by 11 feet, surrounded by four concrete walls. Each cell had a door with a mesh window and a lockable food slot for feeding or passing items through. The bed was originally on the floor on a cement slab, which was later changed to a steel bed suspended above the original bed, and a mattress. Inmates were given institutional blankets and sheets and a pillow.

Any inmate on punishment would lose their mattress and bedding each morning, and would not get it back until the afternoon shift came on duty, approximately eight hours later.

There was a metal bookshelf anchored to the back of the cell as well as a porcelain toilet and basin, all in one, attached to the cement wall. In the corner was a small table and seat, which were also metal and secured to the wall. Inmates were not allowed to have glass containers or anything that could be used as a weapon or self harm; they did not have the use of a fork, knife but were given a spoon at meal times with which to eat their meal. Meals were supplied on a steel tray three times a day along with a metal cup of coffee or juice.

Inmates in the penthouse were locked up approximately 22 hours a day, and given one hour of fresh exercise a day on the roof of the penthouse under strict supervision by an armed guard. They were allowed to shower and clean their cells on a daily basis. They had no TV, but they did have panel on the wall into which they could plug their headphones. It was labelled A for country music, B for rock and roll, and C for a religion.

They were allowed visits, but they were screened, and every inmate who left the penthouse would be in body restraints, which was a chain around their waist along with handcuffs that were attached; he would be accompanied by a guard. Any movement from the penthouse to the visiting area would only happen when the main population was not allowed to move freely around the institution. Once they were returned to the penthouse, they were skinned, frisked, and placed back in their cells.

I remember reporting for afternoon shift one evening. There had been an incident on day shift where an inmate had spit at a guard though his screened window as he passed by his cell. The officer reported what happened to the supervisor in charge of the unit at the time, and the supervisor stated, "Not to worry. We'll take care of that this evening."

The regular complement of staff on duty on afternoon shift was three, consisting of a supervisor and two guards. At around 2100 (9 p.m.) it had been an uneventful night, until the supervisor got up from behind his desk and proceeded to hook the 2-inch fire hose up to a water tap. He then ran the hose down the tier to the cell door of the inmate who had spit at the officer early that day. The supervisor then ordered us to accompany him down the tier. He had in his hand a section of a newspaper. I had no idea what he was planning at the time.

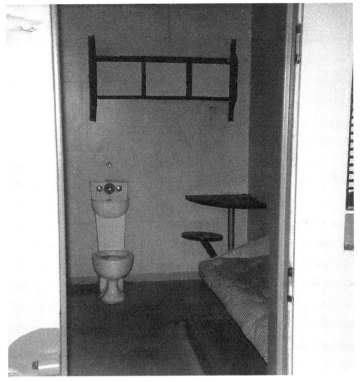

SMSU cell

We then quietly proceeded down the tier, stopping in front of the cell of the inmate who'd spit at the officer on the previous shift. The supervisor then proceeded to light the loose edge of the paper and then tossed it under the door of the cell. It seemed like minutes had passed, and then he kicked the door with his foot, waking up the inmate.

The inmate then started to yell, "Fire! Fire!" As he did, the supervisor aimed the nozzle at the inmate as he lay in his bed and turned on the water. The pressure of the water was pretty intense, and it could almost pin a full-grown man up against the wall. When the water started to run out underneath the cell door, the supervisor shut off the water.

He looked at us, and said, "You did not see a thing. Clean this mess up." Peer pressure was huge back in the day. Being rookies, we were often tasked to perform little tasks to show our solidarity. I never forgot that day. I was not impressed, and I never involved myself in that type of behaviour ever again and would gladly report it—something I made known to my peers.

The old-guard mentality was not going to fade anytime soon. Over the years, some of them eventually got weeded out of the system, but looking back, one can understand why things got heated up within those walls.

INMATE SAYS THERE ARE FECES IN THEIR FOOD

The protective custody unit inmates complained about their food on a regular basis. This was mostly due to the fact that the kitchen workers who were working in the kitchen at the time were from general population. And, of course, anyone who has worked in a split-population institution knows that there is no love lost between them. Given the chance, they constantly battered comments at one another at every opportunity.

In January 1979, they stated that they were finding foreign matter in their food; they believed it was a high possibility that the population inmates were putting human feces into their food. So, on January 7th, they began a demonstration at the supper line. I was on the meal line at the time, standing at the end of the hallway where the inmates picked up their trays. When an inmate threw his tray into the garbage can, the officer standing inside the meal line asked him what the hell he was doing. As a result, a struggle broke out and the officer received numerous bruises to his face. When the struggle was over, approximately a dozen inmates barricaded themselves in the hallway, and the tactical squad was called in to have the area cleared.

It was a constant battle between the main population inmates and the PCU inmates. Eventually, changes were made within the kitchen to ensure that this type of action would not be repeated.

During my 36 years working inside, I always ate the food that came out of the kitchen and never had an issue doing so.

PEN TO CLOSE IN 1980

Since 1948, there had been 26 announcements that the BC Penitentiary was going to close. March 12, 1979, the rumours we heard about closing finally came to fruition. Working in a prison, I found that rumours spread like wildfire; It's just the nature of the beast. We heard that that the old prison might remain open as a protective custody institution or a reception centre. But this was not going to be the case. We were told that it would be closing within three years,

Many of the inmates were not happy about this, as they knew that they would be relocated to the new and high-tech Kent Maximum Institution. They also did not like the idea of moving away from their families and community support.

INMATE KILLED IN GROUP FIGHT

April 27, 1979, the inmates were in the gym for their evening exercise, during which time inmate MacDonald was killed. Previously a armoured car guard, MacDonald was serving time for five years having been charged with the theft of $110 000 after it disappeared from one of the vehicles he was driving.

He was killed after he had been dragged into the gym shower room and beaten by another inmate. The officer in the gym gun cage observed MacDonald trying to crawl out of the gym shower door, only to be kicked and dragged back in by his assailant.

After the gym shower door closed, the officer could no longer see inmate MacDonald. It was only later that the gym shower door opened and a number of inmates ran out. Then two inmates carried MacDonald out and put him on a stretcher, only to have another inmate flip him off it and onto the gym floor.

It took 25 minutes for the officers working in the north wing to get to him after he fell. As the attack was so verbally violent, it sparked the inmates in the north wing to riot in their cells. In total, 41 inmates were charged $80.00 each for damaging their cells; eight inmates were charged in the death of inmate MacDonald, two of whom were serving life sentences. The trial lasted throughout the month of March, ending in three being acquitted, and the jury was unable to reach a verdict on the other five

I was not on duty the evening inmate McDonald was killed in the gym, but I did talk to the officer who was working in the gym gun walk at the time, as well as with the officers working in the north wing that evening. They all said it was something that they would never forget. The screams of pain and anguish that came from inmate McDonald rang out in the north wing dome. They said the sounds he had made chilled them to the bone. It was a cruel and senseless death, but a reminder that life in jail really had no value to some inmates.

MORE ESCAPES

Inmate Bunny Gerein was a high-profile inmate, who was known as an escape artist while I was working in the BC Pen, he was serving a life sentence for the murder of two men. On the 19th of November, he escaped through a hole in the exercise yard at the back of the prison; he left behind a dummy in his cell. He was picked up a week later in a hotel in California; he was on his way back to BC Pen when he managed to slip away from two unarmed deportation officers and was picked again.

Two weeks later, inmate Douceur who was serving seven years for armed robbery, along with inmate McLean, who was waiting trial for murder, escaped while 25 inmates were watching a movie in the gym. The two inmates were able to saw their way through the exit door in the gym, and were well equipped, as they were seen carrying a grappling hook and braided bed sheets for getting over the wall.

ATTRITION

After 1979, the old institution started to wind up. Many of the guards that I worked with were starting to worry about their jobs; many of them felt that they would be on the bottom of the seniority list and would eventually be without a job or unqualified to work in the new high-tech Kent Institution prison. There were rumours around the jail at the time when the notification came out about the closing of the BC Pen, rumours that said the new and upcoming Kent Institution wanted a different kind of guard.

Most of the guards at the BC Pen had worked there for a good many years. Many of them were well-seasoned to the job and used to working under extreme working conditions; the prison was, after all, 102 years old, and would probably fail any health code inspection of today. There were, however, a number of officers who were high profile and those who were always in the centre of things happening around the jail. Most of us were tainted with that negativity of those guards who poked and teased the inmates. And I could understand why the new institution wanted fresh blood, so to speak; many of us just wanted a chance to a fresh start like me.

When I got my job offer, I had three choices: Dorchester and Millhaven prisons, or Kent. Although I was basically a city boy, I really didn't want to transfer to the countryside. In the end, I had no choice, so Kent it was going to be.

GUN DROP

It was February 1980. There were only PCU inmates left in the institution; they were a little more content, as now they had full use of the entire prison without the added pressure of the general population inmates. The atmosphere inside the jail had relaxed a lot, as the PCU population was generally not as violent as the general population inmates. They were a number of them in the TV lounge when a guard accidently dropped his shotgun from his gun cage onto the pool table under him.

I was working in the north wing that day. A few of us were enjoying a cup of coffee and a smoke in the north wing when we heard screaming sounds coming from the lounge. Several of us proceeded up to the entrance for the lounge. We heard the officer in the gun cage yelling at the inmates to back away.

We had no idea that he had dropped his shotgun from the gun cage to the pool table below until one of the inmates told us what was going on. The senior officer with us then ordered the inmates to stand aside as he unlocked the gated steel door and proceeded into the lounge. I noticed the shotgun lying next to the pool table on the floor. The inmates were standing well enough back, taunting the officer in the cage.

The senior officer walked through the crowd of inmates standing around the shotgun, went over and picked it up, and then we all proceeded back the way we had come and reported back to the north wing CX supervisor officer. The officer with the shotgun reported to the main hall to turn the gun into the supervisor on duty.

We found out later what had actually happened. The cage in the lounge had Plexiglass windows all around the lower half of the cage; this was to prevent inmates from throwing stuff up at the officers. The Plexiglass windows were pretty stained from time and were hard to see through. But an inmate cleaner had been escorted up to clean the gun cage and as a result, the Plexiglass windows almost looked invisible. I had worked that post many times over the past few months. Some officers leaned their shotgun up against the Plexiglass as a way to intimidate the inmates.

When the officer got in the cage, he loaded his weapon and went to lean it against the Plexiglass glass. However, he didn't realize that the panel was not fully closed. The shotgun just went through the bars, landed on one of the pool tables under the gun cage, and bounced onto the floor. We all had a good laugh over it, but also realized that it could have gone very badly if one of the inmates had decided to pick it up and use it against us.

It was a moment in time that I will never forget.

PCU INMATES TO KENT

The decision was made, the PCU inmates would be transferred to the new Kent Institution in February; there would be 24 cells for them, and it would be a designated unit within Kent. Then, on February 15, 1990, the last PCU inmate left the 102-year-old prison for Kent Institution. After all was said and done, we had a gala event that was held at the Hyatt Regency Hotel in Vancouver where more than 600 guests honoured the employees of the old penitentiary.

One Tower gun walk

When the last of the PCU inmates were transferred to Kent Institution, a fellow officer took this picture of me on One Tower (left). The one on the right was taken of a fellow officer back in the early 50s on the same tower walkway.

BC PENITENTIARY CLOSES ITS DOORS

For two weeks in May 1980, the prison was opened to the public for the first time. Over 80,000 people attended the open house and a formal ceremony was held to mark the prison closing after 102 years, I had the opportunity to take my father for a personal tour. I remember how concerned he was over the last three years of me working in a maximum security prison, hearing and reading all the media press on the events that took place during my three years there. I remember we were standing in the north wing dorm, and him looking up taking it all in. He then looked at me and said, "So why are they closing it, it looks like a pretty nice jail to me."

What my father did not know, was that the government had previously spent thousands of dollars fixing it up for the public to see it, the public never saw the bird shit what was heaped up on the bars of most of the north and south wings or the parade of mice that haunted the tiers of the prison. The BC Penitentiary had served its purpose, being outdated and slowly falling apart, it was time to move to the next maximum security level of prison.

CHAPTER 5

KENT INSTITUTION

Kent Institution opened in 1979, and is the only maximum security federal penitentiary in the Correctional Service of Canada in the Pacific region (BC). It housed 298 inmates at the time and was located in the district of Kent, between Agassiz and Harrison Hot Springs BC.

It was nicked named "the big house." The place were bad boys go, it was going to be home for the country's worst offenders: serial killers, sex slayers, child molesters, and violent robbers.

It was one of the first institutions to have the Living Unit Program. What this really meant was officers who worked in the units would be in civilian clothing instead of uniform.

I transferred to Kent Institution as a Correctional Officer-I (CO-I) in May of 1980 after BC Penitentiary officially closed. It was an impressive sight to see. Instead of four concrete walls, it had two double-wide fences topped off with razor wire surrounding the whole entire institution. In addition, there were four modern guard towers, along with a motor patrol vehicle that patrolled around the institution 24 hours a day, seven days a week.

It was the Correctional Service of Canada's (CSC) new high-tech institution, equipped with electronic gates and doors, bulletproof glass, and electronic monitored fences. In the central control room, buried deep inside Kent's thick walls, was a correctional officer who watched a number of video monitors. He could see inside the kitchen, the washrooms, the hallways and fence line. He watched and recorded everything. There were more than 30 eyes in the sky, and staff and inmates were watched 24 hours a day. Throughout the institution there were "bubbles"—well-secured areas where correctional officers had a bird's eye view of the cell blocks. The officer was locked in and he let no one in or out without permission. Each bubble is equipped with port holes he could shoot out of, if the need arose.

Officers would access these posts through the main tunnel that runs under the institution. The tunnel also allowed staff and emergency response teams to respond to areas, instead of having to go through inmate-populated areas of the institution.

HOSPITAL CONTROL

I was working the first half of my afternoon shift in hospital control. We had just finished the inmate supper line, and recreation was next on the schedule. Hospital control can be a very busy post, as you have three main doors that control movement in and out of the gym, courtyard, and programs corridor, as well as four electronic doors.

I had just let the inmates into the gym, and movement had ceased. I locked down my area, and thought, *What a great time to get a coffee and enjoy the peace and quiet for a little while.* The gym had two recreational officers who worked in plainclothes. This shift, I noticed that they were shorthanded, and one of them was our Institutional Training Officer, Gerry Enright, who was working overtime in the gym.

During my years at Kent, Gerry Enright was one of the best training officers that I ever had the pleasure to be trained under. He was a retired Chief Warrant Officer with the Royal Canadian Regiment and had served in the Canadian military for over 27 years. I had just made my coffee and was returning to my control console, when I heard someone shaking the gym gate. I looked over and I could see Gerry waving through the bars at me. I opened the gate wide enough for him to walk through, and closed it behind him. He immediately walked over to my bubble, and I could sense that something was a little off, as he wasn't his usual jolly self. Before I could ask him anything, he blurted out, "There has been a stabbing in the inmates' gym bathroom."

"Okay," I said. "Are you okay, and is everything okay in the office?"

"Yes," he responded

So I said, "Go back to the gym office and lock it behind you. I'll call central and let them know right away."

As soon as Gerry was back in the gym, I called central and informed them of what he had told me. Within minutes there were about a dozen correctional officers in my area, waiting direction from the correctional supervisor as what to do next. Two officers were assigned to pick up a gurney and escort the nurse into the gym. I was instructed to open the gym gate, and the supervisor and nurse, escorted by six correctional officers, entered the gymnasium. I locked the gym gate behind them and was instructed not to allow any movement unless it was staff.

About 12 minutes later, the keeper was banging on the hospital gate. I opened it and could see an inmate on the gurney in a black and white T-shirt. The nurse was doing chest compressions on him as they were moving him. It was apparent that he had been stabbed pretty aggressively because every time the nurse did chest compressions, the inmate's black and white shirt became more saturated with his own blood.

I opened the hospital doors, as an ambulance was waiting at the back door of the hospital. The inmate was 25-year-old Dean Thomas Langford, who had been sentenced to life for the stabbing and killing of two Aboriginal sisters who lived in Sooke, BC in 1979.

A week earlier, I had been in Admission and Discharge when inmate Langford was being processed. There were some concerns about him going into general population. This was shared with him during his admission process. It was highly recommended he sign himself into protective custody, but he refused, choosing the main prison population.

It was no surprise as to what happened to him. When first admitted, he had an attitude from the get-go and thought he was tough. He was very young, and actually had no idea of what maximum security was all about. As a result of his death, three inmates were charged with his murder.

MEALTIME

I remember one incident while working on monitoring the kitchen entrance where the inmates entered for supper. I and another officer were standing outside of the kitchen industries control bubble, which led to the industrial area of the institution. We were there to open the door to the inmates' dining room, monitor the movement of inmates, and control any contraband in and out of the inmate dining room. We would peek in occasionally to ensure that everything was quiet.

I remember telling this young, inexperienced officer not to stand by the doorway and stare at the inmates while they are eating. As I am sure you would agree, you wouldn't like someone staring at you while you are eating. He ignored my advice, and as it turned out, there was an inmate sitting at a table relatively close to the kitchen door who was well-known to be emotionally unstable and violent on several occasions.

The next thing I knew, I could hear this inmate yelling at the officer, "Hey, asshole. What the fuck are you looking at?"

Again, I asked the officer to step back, away from the doorway. At the time, I was standing across from the kitchen door, observing the meal line. My back was next to the cement wall right beside the bubble.

The inmate stood up. His posturing was more pronounced as he again yelled at the officer. "What the hell is your problem, asshole?"

Next thing I saw was the inmate reaching to the middle of a table next to him. He picked up a bottle of HP sauce, and the next thing I saw was him standing right in my line of sight. He hurled it in our direction.

My instincts made me duck at the very last second, as the bottle passed by the officer's face and smashed on the wall directly above my head. I then immediately went up to the kitchen door and slammed it shut, locking it to isolate us from our attacker.

The back of my uniform shirt and neck were splattered with HP sauce. The inmate threw it with such force that when the bottle hit the wall above my head, it had completely disintegrated. there was nothing left of the glass bottle, other than the lid, which lay some 20 feet from where it exploded on the wall.

The officer in the bubble immediately called central control, and a team of about six officers came to our rescue within minutes of his call. We took a few minutes before unlocking the kitchen door and calling the inmate out to our location, he was told that he was going to segregation and would be charged.

His response: "I don't like to be stared at while eating my dinner!" He was cuffed and escorted to the segregation unit. I thank my lucky stars that I ducked at the last second.

CHRISTMAS DAY

It was December 25, 1980: Christmas Day. I was working afternoon shift in the A&B bubble, the control centre for both A and B units. These bubbles are best described as working inside a large aquarium. There was an unrestricted view of the ranges up and down both units, with gun ports facing every tier. Each unit housed 24 inmates, 12 up and 12 down. The uniformed officers were responsible for controlling the cell doors and access in and out of the unit.

It was suppertime, and like every Christmas, it consisted of turkey dinner with all the trimmings, along with ice cream and assorted fruit. Fruit was commonly used to make brews. (They conjured up homemade alcohol using fruit, sugar, and bread, which acted like yeast. Never underestimate the innovative capabilities of a caged person!)

Officers working the units were instructed by the head living unit officer to check each cell and to remove any excess of fruit that they found. This normally meant that the inmates were allowed two pieces of fruit. The Christmas season was always a touchy time of year. We were always on edge since emotions were high on both sides of the bars during the holiday season.

The living unit officers in a unit were making their rounds and anytime they were there, it was the officer in the bubble's responsibility to monitor their movement while on the tier. They came off the upper range with an armful of oranges and apples, and then returned to their office and then proceeded to make their rounds of the lower unit. Once completed, they returned to their office with another armful of fruit. It was not long after their round that an inmate walked off the upper range and proceeded to the living unit office. I was not aware at the time, but one of the officers was eating a tangerine orange in the office.

The inmate became very verbal and stated yelling, "What the hell is this? You come search our rooms, take our fruit, and then sit there on your fat ass and eat it!"

The inmate got more aggressive in his actions, escalating the argument between him and the officers.

My focus was totally on the situation, observing the yelling inmate inciting others in the unit. Things started to get ugly very quickly.

I called central control, telling them of the situation at hand. I was instructed to keep an eye on things with assistance on the way.

As I hung up the phone, I could see inmates getting more and more agitated and gathering outside the living unit office hollering, "If you want it, then have it all!"

They proceeded to take the wooden shelves storing new papers and paperback books that were kept against the wall outside the unit office, stacking them in the office doorway. I could no longer see into the office. I immediately called them on the phone, asking how they were doing. The only response was I got back was some mumbling. I told the living unit officer, "Hang on. Help is on the way."

I immediately called central control and said, "Send help," then hung up the phone.

One of the inmates had a book of matches in his hand. "Let's burn them to the ground!"

Immediately I opened the gun slot facing the living unit office, and grasped my .38 revolver with my right hand.

The inmate lit his book of matches on fire. Next, he heard my command, "Stop, or I will shoot." I had drawn my revolver and cocked the hammer back. He looked directly at me and down the barrel of my .38 and froze.

"Step back away from the office door and drop the matches."

He slowly stepped back from the office door, not realizing the match book was burning down towards his fingers. He shook his hand and dropped the burning matches, hitting the floor at the same time. Just at that moment, there was a banging at the inner door to the unit. I looked over to see that it was filled with officers, led by the correctional supervisor on duty. Help had finally arrived.

Being left-handed, I had to move my revolver over to my right hand, and then leaned over to the panel to open the door.

The supervisor noticed that I still had my weapon pointed through the gun port. He kept everybody back and said, "It's okay. Lock the upper and lower tier doors. We've got it from here."

I then withdrew my revolver, placing the hamper on safe mode, and holstered my weapon. I returned to the door panel and closed the upper and lower tier doors as the response team filtered into the unit.

They cuffed the pyromania-inclined inmate, escorting him to segregation. The other officers cleared out the bookshelves and checked on the living unit officer in the office.

I didn't notice at the time, but my hands had started shaking a little, so I sat down in my chair to catch my breath. The supervisor came to my gun port window telling me I was going to relieved. When I proceeded to central control, my hands were shaking all the way. I found out later that the living unit officer in the office had been eating fruit brought from home.

Your typical Christmas Day in the big house.

LIVING UNIT OFFICER

On May 29, 1981, I successfully completed screening to become a living unit officer. I was assigned to H unit.

The living unit system was first introduced into Kent in 1979. It was the Correctional Service of Canada's way of integrating non-uniform correctional officers into a new concept. The old system of fences and steel bars to maintain control were still in effect; but the new catch phrase was "dynamic security."

The intention was to establish positive interpersonal relations between staff and inmates and was a critical component in operating the new prison system. Each living unit officer would be assigned a small caseload of inmates in his unit.

The living unit officer would be responsible for reviewing files on every inmate assigned to him, along with completing monthly reports on inmates on his case load, including the inmates' progress or lack thereof. It was believed at the time that removing the uniform would ease the tension between the inmates and the old-guard attitude. Problem was, you can take the uniform off the guard, but attitudes remain the same.

It was effective to a point, but the whole concept needed time for staff to adapt into the new system.

The old-guard mentality had to be flushed. Changes were never easy for many officers. People get comfortable in a routine and a particular mindset. But, in time, things changed, and it wasn't really the uniform that made the changes; it was the staff's attitude.

We walked the tiers every day, all day. For many of us it was like policing our own little community. Interaction with the inmates was the focus that worked rather well. I would come on day shift, and when I did my count in the morning on the range, I would often say good morning to the inmates. It took them awhile to get used to it, but eventually most of them would respond back.

LIVING UNIT OFFICER JOB DESCRIPTION

Living unit officers, under the direction of the living unit supervisor, are responsible for the security of the unit and for the care and custody of the inmates within that unit. These security duties, which must be performed in adherence to the institutional standing orders and the rules and regulations of the unit, include: counts, security checks, fire checks, rounds, checks of locks and barriers, frisks, searches, key control, and removal of inmates to dissociation. Dissociation is a secure unit, isolated from the main population units and inmates, and is seldom used. Its purpose is to protect an inmate from those in population who would do them harm, or to protect those inmates who have been threatened by other inmates and need to be segregated from the main population. Dissociation was usually just temporary, until a decision could be made later as what to do with them.

The main reason that I applied for the living unit officer position was the simple fact that I like the new challenges and I did not like to be confined to locked security posts. The idea of no longer wearing a uniform was also attractive. Plus, the added advantage of being free to move around the institution at will was a bonus.

KENT INSTITUTION RIOT, JUNE 1981

On my first day as a living unit officer, I looked forward to moving more freely around the institution as I did not like being confined in the control posts. I was well aware that there had been a riot at the institution the night before. I arrived to work that morning to an institution that was just buzzing.

There were a number of uniform personnel in the briefing room—a mix of emergency response officers as well as non-uniform staff. The morning briefing was going to be held in the Visits and Correspondence area, due to the number present. We were briefed on the current situation.

There were about 103 inmates presently camping out in the exercise field. They would remain there until the inmates elected a negotiation committee to act in their behalf. I was assigned to kitchen industries control post with another officer. I was definitely not happy about being contained in a bubble on my first day as a living unit officer. When I arrived at my assigned post, I called the head living unit officer and requested to be assigned to a unit. I really didn't want to be locked up in a bubble when things were happing in the jail. In the end, I was assigned to the gym, where we would be armed and were assigned to monitor the inmates in the yard.

The riot happened around 16:00 (4 p.m.). The inmates were released for dinner, and staff reported that about a half hour later, banging and yelling was heard coming from across the courtyard. The staff managed to get some of the unit's barriers closed, but A, B, C, and D units were not so lucky. The inmates managed to breach A-B control posts with a weight bar taken from the gym. Most of the living unit staff were able to get to G, E, and F units after being warned by the inmates to get the hell out of their respective units.

At around 18:20 (6:20 p.m.), it all erupted almost simultaneously in the units and the gymnasium, during the time that the inmates were in the exercise yard. Four inmates were injured. Several others suffered minor injuries. Two were stabbed. During one of the stabbing assaults, the officer in the tower fired, grazing the inmate, who was taken to the hospital having received minor injuries.

The units were damaged from smoke and some from tear gas that was used during the riot. My first impression of the prison post-riot was overwhelming. It is amazing how, in such a short period of time (within two hours), so much damage could be done.

The inmates eventually cleaned up the units. Work crews were assigned to those areas that needed to be cleaned. Some units were okay, but some others need construction work and glass replacement. In the end, everything slowly started to get back to normal.

RAIN COOLS INMATES AFTER RIOT

Chilliwack Progress, June 10, 1981

By Ron Gray

After a two-hour $100,000 binge of breaking and burning Sunday night, 103 inmates of Kent prison spent nearly 40 hours huddled outdoors without food.

During about half that time, rain soaked their improvised tent city on the south playing field while they glared sullenly at the living units they had ravaged.

Warden John Dowsett said a "quick estimate" of the damage to the maximum security jail was about $100,000.

No serious structural damage was done to the building, he said.

Living units would soon be habitable, Dowsett said, but "they'll have to clean them up," he growled.

Four inmates were injured. A few others were treated for minor illness and sent back to the playing field.

Two were stabbed "numerous times" around the head and neck; one of them was also stabbed in the chest, shoulder and back; the other was tabbed at least once in the abdomen.

Both were taken to Shaughnessy Hospital in Vancouver where they treated in surgery. One of the men was undergoing a second operation later yesterday afternoon.

During the assault on the second stabbing victim, an alleged assailant was felled by a bullet from a prison guard's rifle, which grazed his head.

He was taken to hospital where he recovered consciousness and received stitches for a minor wound.

The discipline incident that some staff thought triggered the trouble occurred at 4 p.m. Sunday, when two inmates who were fighting were taken to the segregation unit.

Some inmates arranged a meeting at 5:30 p.m. in the courtyard, a common procedure for squelching rumors at Kent.

"The feeling of an inmate and some staff members I talked to, was that the meeting succeeded in cooling things down," said corrections spokesman Jack Stewart.

At 6 p.m., as inmates were on their way from the dining room to normal evening recreation activities: some were headed into the yard, some to cells to read, some to living unit recreation areas to play pool or watch television.

At 6:22, in what officials believe was a co-ordinated action, violence erupted.

It started almost simultaneously in the west wing living units and in the gymnasium.

Prison staff were not threatened; inmates warned several of them to leave.

Mats in the gymnasium were set ablaze. Windows were smashed all along the west wing. The barber shop was torched and the canteen looted of all kinds of stock, even soap. Candy bars were strewn about the corridor.

In the living units, there was very little attempt to damage the cells, although some mattresses were burned. But pool table and televisions in the recreation areas were smashed, and 11 of the 12 living unit offices were put to the torch.

The bar from a weight lifters bar-bell was used to smash inch-thick bullet-proof glass in the control "bubbles" of the west wing.

Inmates actually broke into the bubble that controls living units A and B, and opened cell doors. But no damage was done to the complex electronic control panel in the bubble. They were later routed with tear gas.

At about 8 p.m., the order to vacate the wing was given over a loud-hailer, and 107 inmates immediately began to move out. Many took parkas with them.

By 8:15 p.m. Sunday the staff had again secured control of the west wing.

Authorities are not able to say why, but neither of the two general population units in the east wing attempted to join the fray. The other two east wing units are segregation and protective custody: inmates there were confined throughout.

The two stabbings occurred on the south playing field, sometime between 9:30 and 10:30 p.m.

A fourth inmate left the exercise yard and came into the prison building with a broken jaw.

Staff were advised that some inmates suffered minor buckshot wounds from warning shots fired to discourage attempts to break the floodlights with stones; band-aids were provided for these and for the inmates with glass cuts from the broken windows.

The inmates spent the rest of Sunday night and all day Monday in the playing field.

Warden John Dowsett rejected the first parlay bid from the rioters, and set his conditions for talks: he would talk with an inmate or inmate committee deemed "reasonable"; he required all inmates to submit to a search for weapons and contraband; and he required a list of 24 "acceptable" volunteers for clean-up duty in the living units.

At 10 a.m. yesterday, the inmates complied. They named a committee of three.

An electronic search was made for weapons on the north field. Then inmates were taken into the auditorium for a skin frisk.

After being searched, they were sent to the north playing field where coffee and sandwiches were waiting — their first food in 38 hours or more.

When the searches were over and a variety of weapons and contraband recovered, the south playing field was searched, and more illegal possessions retrieved.

Then the inmates were returned to the south field where they were supplied with plastic sheets to improvise tents, and firewood to build bonfires.

Stewart said one of the costly areas of damage is the gymnasium floor. That and furniture and recreation equipment will probably be replaced by proceeds from the inmate fund, Stewart said.

A portion of wages earned by the inmates goes into that fund automatically.

Most of the furniture can be built in the prison's own shops by inmate labor for only the cost of materials, said Stewart.

Work was to begin yesterday on the cleanup of the living units, but there was no estimate of the time required to make them livable.

Work on the common rooms and gymnasium will not be tackled until a later date, said assistant warden Tony Hawkins.

FIRST FEMALE CORRECTIONAL OFFICERS ARRIVE

At my arrival to the penitentiary service in 1977, there were no female correctional officers working in maximum security institutions. It was not until around the early 80s that we were informed that Kent Institution would soon to be receiving six new female officers assigned to security posts within the Institution.

This was met with more than a little resistance from a good many of my fellow officers, many who had their own personal valid concerns and voiced then openly.

Women are physically weaker than men and would be of little use in any sort of physical confrontation with offenders. This would also endanger staff who were morally and professionally obligated to protect them.

Women would be at an undeniable high risk of being physically assaulted or raped by inmates who had been proven to be predatory and were sexually deprived.

Women might become emotionally or sexually involved with inmates and compromise their positions as correctional officers.

Women would have limited use on walking the ranges because of inmate privacy issues, and would not be able to conduct strip searches, thus increasing male officers' workloads.

Personally, I didn't believe that maximum security was a suitable place for female officers. Medium and minimum security institutions would be more suitable.

Nevertheless, the management team handpicked six female officers to work at Kent Institution. All the new female officers had prior history of working in provincial women-only jails and at the start, resistance from my male counterparts lessened somewhat once they arrived. Of course, there were bad taste jokes and a few of them got left nasty notes in their mailboxes such as "Go home to your husband."

But they withstood the peer pressure from their male counterparts and in the end, they were accepted and became well suited to working at Kent Institution.

Those first women corrections officers opened doors for more to follow, and my opinion changed.

My last few years as a living unit officer at Kent, I had the honour to have worked with a woman who transferred in from the Prairie Region. She was an outstanding corrections officer, having seen her fair share of death and dismay during her career. Over the next few years, we developed a great working relationship. I came to admire her for who she was as a person and professional. I had great faith in her and her personal instincts. She developed rapport with the inmates, earning respect for her and I confided in her on many occasions.

I always knew that she had my back when we were walking the ranges and on the job.

In the end, the consensus was women officers varied little from male officers. They do their jobs in a different manner. Their presence softens the prison environment since most of the male inmates in the institution had to adapt to their new authority figures. This in turn coaxed the male population on both sides of the bars to revisit traditional attitudes where women were formerly stereotyped as housekeepers and subordinates.

I was not shocked to find out that male inmates would often discuss things with a female officer that they would not normally discuss with male officers, including sharing personal relationships with their girlfriends and wives.

In the years that followed co-staffing, the decision to implement female officers into a dominated male environment had its ups and downs; although, in the end it, appeared that the rewards of a both gender prisons' staffing policies far outweighed the added managerial burdens that the policy might have incurred.

MOTORCYCLE CLUB: BLUE KNIGHTS BC V

The year was 1985; there were a number of officers who rode motorcycles to work during the summer, including myself. We were sitting around the office, having our morning coffee, when someone brought up the idea of starting our own motorcycle club.

One of the officers mentioned that there was already a club out there called the Blue Knights, which as it turned out was a non-profit fraternal organization consisting of active and retired law enforcement officers who enjoy riding motorcycles. The Blue Knights originally started out in Bangor, Maine, USA, by a small group of police officers who formed what is known today as an international motorcycle club.

As it turned out there were four chapters in BC, and the closest was in Vancouver. It was decided among us that we should start our own chapter for the Fraser Valley, and so we contacted the Vancouver chapter to find out how to make this happen.

Long story short: we started our own chapter, BC V, based in Chilliwack, BC; our club originally consisted of mostly correctional officers. Over time, we grew to around 30 members, including members from the RCMP, sheriff's department, and parole officers.

During my five years as president, we contributed to many events, such as escorting Steve Fonyo, who was a Canadian athlete and finished Terry Fox's run across Canada, raising millions for cancer research. We were his person motorcycle escort from Hope to Abbotsford.

We contributed as well as Rick Hansen's personal motorcycle escort from Hope to Abbotsford. Hansen was known for his Man in Motion World Tour, which was inspired by Terry Fox's Marathon of Hope,

I attended many Blue Knight events over the years; one, which was my personal favourite,was the Abbotsford Toy Run, which was held every year in the fall. This was a traditional event in which each motorcycle rider would buy a new toy that would be donated to a charity for distribution to children in need at Christmas.

During one such event, we attended the Chilliwack Christmas parade through downtown, and then headed down to Abbotsford to where other motorcycles and other clubs would be gathering. I was leading our club as the president at the time; we had approximately 25 motorcycles in attendance. One of our members took his trailer, which he pulled behind his bike and converted it into a Santa sled, which included a set of fake antlers on the front if his bike. In the trailer was a large stuffed animal; it was pretty awesome to see, and it got a lot of attention from everyone who saw it.

We pulled into the parking lot, and I could see that there was an opening for the number of our members just ahead. as I started to pull up; I noticed that we would be parking next to a chapter of the Hells Angels.

As I pulled up and stopped my bike, I heard a loud snarky voice yell out, "Oh, look. The pigs are here with their toys." Then the man laughed out loud.

I thought, *Oh, now this is going to be interesting.* As I was swinging off my bike, I heard a large thud sound, like someone hitting someone in the face. Once off my bike, I turned around to look over to where the sound came from. I saw this very large bearded man, dressed in leathers, standing over someone who was at the time laying on the ground at the bearded man's feet. I could see that he was a full patch member. He looked over at me and said. "Sorry about that, sir. It won't happen again." A sigh of relief came over me as I really didn't want to get into a confrontation, so I just smiled at him, and said, "We are all good, thanks." Then we proceeded to the meeting hall with everyone else.

I was president of BC V for some five years, and a member for eight. I travelled throughout British Columbia and the United States, and one time a group of us headed down to California to Tijuana, Mexico and back up the Oregon coast. It was and still is a part something that I enjoy doing even to this day. I enjoy the feeling of freedom that it gives me, along with the friendships and brotherhood it created for me. Not to mention that riding a motorcycle takes away all the tension and stress and gives you a reboot— that's the best way that I can describe it.

Although I am no longer a member of the Blue Knights, I have fond memories of my time in the club, and it was an experience of a lifetime that I will never forget.

INTRODUCTION TO THE MOB

I was talking to my mother one Sunday evening. She informed me her former husband and my stepfather had been suffering for years with Parkinson's disease. He was not doing well.

I hadn't talked to him in a very long time, so the next morning, I called his office and his secretary remembered who I was since I had visited his union office on more than one occasion in the past. She gave me Uncle John's number and I called him right away. He sounded a little different on the phone since we last talked. We talked for a bit and we agreed to do dinner that Saturday.

We arranged to meet at his home in Vancouver's West End. I was a little taken aback by the sight of him as he greeted me at the door. He was not the stocky, hearty man I remembered. Instead, he was about half his weight and a lot greyer; but he still that same proud persona that I knew in my twenties.

He wanted to know about my life, and what I had been doing. I told him that I was a correctional officer at Kent Institution and had been for the past five years. He looked at me over his glasses and said, "Do you know a guy in there called Fats Robertson?"

I said, "Sure, everyone does. He's a strong influence among the inmates and rumour is he pretty much runs the jail."

He just chuckled, and said, "Oh, no doubt there. Next time you see him, tell him Johnny C says hi."

We spent the evening taking about his new wife. He wanted to know how my sister was and hoped my mom was happy. He was a man of mystery sometimes, but was always good to my sister and myself. I always had the outmost respect for him. I returned home that evening, as I had to report for day shift the next day. I arrived at work, then reported to my unit. It was a quiet day and at noon I headed over to the kitchen to have lunch.

One of the best jobs an inmate in jail can have is working in the kitchen. At the now-defunct BC Penitentiary, staff had a private dining room with food served by contract civilian staff. Some of my fellow officers would have you believe that the inmates put stuff in our food. Personally, I never got sick while working there or at any other institution that I worked in.

At Kent, we also had our own dining room as well, served by an inmate behind a steam table. The inmate who had the privilege of serving us had had the post for a good number of years. It was well-known that particular person pretty much governed the inmate population.

This was the infamous "Fats Robertson" my stepfather knew. He was serving a minimum of 15 years for importing drugs into Canada. Apparently, Fats had brought contraband drugs into Vancouver's harbour for years before getting caught in by long arm of the law.

I arrived at the dining room, happy to see that there were not a lot of people, and got in line behind fellow officers. Inmate Robertson was serving lunch. I was last in line and, stepping up to the serving area, asked, "So, what's good?"

He said, "Everything as usual", and laughed.

As he was putting lunch on my tray, I said, "Oh, by the way. A friend of yours says 'Hi.' Johnny C, from Vancouver."

He didn't bat an eye or say a word. Just smiled and said, "Enjoy!"

I joined my fellow officers at the nearest table.

A few days later, I was back in the kitchen a little late then normal and noticed the noon-hour rush was on and the dining room was packed with correctional and institutional personnel. I had gotten in line for the steam table when inmate Robertson looked at me and to my surprise reached across the top of the steam table to shake my hand.

I was shocked; in all my years working, I had never had an inmate shake my hand. I didn't know what to do, so I returned the friendly gesture.

Fats looked at me smiling and said, "You're Johnny C's son, who served in the Navy."

I had no idea what to do or say next and my first response was to look around the room and see who observed me shake his hand. But no one did. It went completely unnoticed, which was a sigh of relief. Fraternization with inmates was not looked upon very kindly by other officers and was clearly lined out in the CSC policy of what those infractions were.

As I was putting my food on my tray, he said, "Not to worry. As long as you are working in Kent, you will have an umbrella over you."

I just nodded at him and went to find a place to sit down and have my lunch. Suddenly, I was not so hungry. I was now thinking, *I have to put this to the Institutional Preventative Security Office (IPSO)*, as it was something that needed to be on record.

I was confused by what Fats meant by his statement. Then it finally clicked. Being around inmates for as long as I had at this point in my career, I shook it off as inmate babble. As I was sitting in the unit office, I began writing my report in detail, including the conversation that I had with my uncle in Vancouver. When my partner returned shortly after, I had finished it and I told him that I had to go drop off a report with the Institutional Preventive Security Office. I personally knew one of the IPSO officers pretty well.

Scott was sitting behind his desk working. I sat down and handed him my report telling him, "There's a situation I find hard to believe." I told him everything and he listened attentively taking it all in.

His response: "Wow, that's interesting. Sounds like your stepfather was in the mob, but let us know if anything else more develops."

DUH.

Nothing more was said between inmate Robertson and me in that regard; most of the time he kept to himself. But we did occasionally nod at one another in passing on the unit or in the courtyard. While he was living in my unit, it was exceptionally quiet, and was the very first unit in Kent to get a colour TV, purchased through the institution, and paid for by him. It was only watched by his select group; of course.

During the 1981 riot, his TV was smashed by an inmate new to our unit. When the inmates were out in the yard, he was caught bragging about it. It wasn't long after the inmates entered the yard that the newbie inmate came out from the back of the gym complaining about a broken arm. He said he fell. We all pretty much guessed what had happened.

We had one of the cleanest units in the institution at that time, with next to zero trouble with any of the inmates. It was also pretty much crime-free for the most part, with us only finding the occasional brews stashed away. But not on Fats' floor, as his leadership was apparent.

MY MISSING COFFEE MUG

One afternoon shift, after the evening count, we opened up to let inmates report to the gym. I grabbed a coffee and headed to visit a fellow officer working in the gym at the same time. I left the gym a little later, returning to my unit, but realized I had left my coffee mug in the gym office.

It was kind of special to me as it had been a Christmas gift from my wife. I immediately turned around and headed back to fetch it. But when I arrived, it was not to be found and my first thought was an inmate took a liking to it, never to be seen again. Some weeks later I was once again on day shift and as I was waiting to be served lunch by inmate Robertson, he reached under the counter and to my astonishment he put my coffee mug on the top of the steam table saying, "I believe this belongs to you, Cookie."

I felt right uncomfortable mostly because I didn't know what to say, so I just thanked him, got my lunch, and carried on with my day. Now I had to file another report when I returned to my unit.

Years after I left Kent, when conversing with my mother, she told me that she had suspected that something was up with Uncle John. Seeing that she never really knew anything, she just kept her thoughts to herself.

A CASE OF MISTAKEN IDENTITY

My partner and I were working in H unit one evening when the duty supervisor informed us there was an incident in the gym. They were going to announce over the PA system to have all inmates return to their units. Once inmate movement was over, we did the lock up and conducted a count.

Once the count was completed, my partner and I noted that one of our inmates was missing, Frank Laronde. Frank was a well-seasoned, somewhat hardened inmate who had been incarcerated most of his life. He knew his way around the jail and was known to be a bad boy in his day. He was generally respected by the majority of the inmate population, and reasonably respectful when dealing with staff. But he was also savvy, knowing where to draw the line.

A few days prior to the gym incident, I was doing a range walk on the tier where Frank lived. I could hear a buzzing sound coming from his tier. I walked up to his cell door and saw him sitting on the foot of his bed, looking out his window while another inmate, who was a well-known tattoo artist, was working on a tattoo on Frank's forearm.

I stood in his doorway for about five seconds before clearing my throat, and then said out loud, "Someone needs to fire their six man. A "six man" is another inmate who keeps watch out for guards doing their rounds on the tier; usually saying out loud the word six warning other inmates that guards are close.

I stepped into Frank's cell, to take a look at the tattoo in progress: an outlined silhouette of a wolf. To the inmate doing the tattoo, I said, "I'll take that tattoo gun, if you don't mind."

He didn't argue with me. He just turned around and handed it over. Seeing that both inmates lived in the unit and never gave staff a bad time, I decided to just junk that tattoo gun. Innovation yet again: it was made out of parts from a portable stereo.

Once the count was done and all the inmates were locked up, we soon realized that we were short one, that one being inmate Laronde. It was soon after that that we got the news of a murder in the gym.

I headed to the gym and once I reached the Hospital Control post, I walked up to the bubble and said to the officer inside the bubble, "Let me in." I was closely accompanied by a new officer, who was standing outside the bubble. We both hustled into the gymnasium and right away I could see a gym officer standing outside the music room door, where inmates who played instruments could go to practice in private.

Right there in the centre of the music room was a body lying in a pool of blood. The smell of fresh blood filled the room. The new officer next to me turned a little white and said, "I think I'm going to hurl." I told the rookie CO to head to the washroom two doors down and off he went. My instinctual forensic skill set noticed the blood-soaked baseball bat lying close to the body. It didn't take much figuring out to know what happened.

Then, I noticed the tattoo on Frank's lifeless forearm from the other day. It was learned later that Frank's death was a case of mistaken identity. Frank was bludgeoned to death by a young inmate by the name of Skinner, who was serving a five-year sentence for repeated break and enters. The jail house gossip at the time was Skinner was hired to kill someone, who looked a lot like Frank, over some drug deal gone badly. Skinner was charged, convicted, and sentenced for the murder of Frank Laronde.

I left the music room to check on how the new officer was. He was shaken a little. I told him I was sorry he had to see that, but it was after all, the workplace environment.

KENT ON LOCKDOWN ONCE AGAIN: JANUARY 27, 1988

This was my second riot, once again Kent Institution was on "lockdown." it all began at around 17:00 (5 p.m.), during the inmate supper feeding, and about 85 inmates were in the dining room at the time when a fight broke out between two inmates.

There were five correctional officers in the dining room. When the fight began, the officers attempted to break up the fight and were as a result assaulted. The officer in the kitchen gun walk fired a warning shot, which distracted the inmates long enough to give the correctional officers enough time to escape the dining room and secure it.

Two food service officers, who were in the kitchen at the time, were also able lock themselves in the staff dining room and were able to get out into the main courtyard, where they were met and escorted safety by correctional officers.

The inmates were able to break into the officers' dining room, and wreak havoc, breaking dishes and smashing everything they could get their hands on.

The emergency response team was called in. The inmates were ordered to leave the dining room, but refused, so tear gas was used. The inmates vacated the kitchen area and gathered in the courtyard, where they were met by the emergency response team and escorted back to their respective units, two at a time.

By 21:00 (9 p.m.), it was all over. In total, about 100 to 110 inmates were involved and an excessive amount of damages occurred to the kitchen and dining areas; as well, one inmate was stabbed and sent to the hospital.

KENT ON LOCKDOWN FOLLOWING RIOT

Chilliwack Progress, January 27, 1988

By Michelle Mallette

Kent institution's 240 inmates are on "lockdown" following a two-hour riot at the maximum security federal prison Sunday evening.

About $20,000 worth of damage occurred to the prison kitchen and dining area, and inmates are now receiving two cold meals a day with the kitchen out of commission.

The incident began at about 5 p.m., during the supper hour. Judy Croft, assistant warden of management services, said about 85 inmates were in the dining area when a fight broke out between two prisoners.

Five correctional officers were in the dining area at the time, and Croft said they moved in to break up the fight.

Another scuffle broke out nearby, and when the guards, moved to break up that fight, "they were assaulted," Croft said.

"The officer in the gun walk, which is above the dining area, fired a warning shot into the air," she said. The shot "startled" the inmates and gave the guards enough time to escape and lock the dining area.

Two food service employees, who were in the kitchen at the time, locked the kitchen door, entered the staff dining room and locked that door, and finally locked themselves inside an office adjacent to the staff dining area.

"They phoned Central (Control) and told us where they were. Twenty minutes to a half hour later they heard the smashing up (in the kitchen area). They heard the destruction begin," Croft said.

The kitchen workers left the office through a door into the courtyard, where they were met by guards who escorted them to safety.

"The inmates (eventually) broke into the kitchen, the staff dining area and the office. They broke plates, dropped food, broke windows; just general destruction," Croft told The Progress.

Croft said one inmate was stabbed and sustained a punctured lung. He was transferred to a Vancouver hospital for treatment.

"When they broke the window from the dining room into the courtyard . . . we advised them that if they did not all come out we would (tear) gas the kitchen and dining area," Croft said.

Tear gas was used, forcing the prisoners still in the kitchen area into the courtyard.

By then, the prison's emergency response (ERT) team was in place around the main courtyard. The inmates were ordered to spread themselves against a wall, and were moved, "two by two," into their living units where they were strip-searched for weapons before being locked up.

It took the ERT team about 1½ hours to move all the inmates into their cells.

"It was over at about 9 o'clock," Croft said.

In total, about 100 to 110 inmates were involved, including those in the courtyard when the riot broke out.

SURROUNDED BY INMATES

It was November 10, 1989, 18:15 (6:15 p.m.). I was working in B unit at the time. I received a phone call from the correctional supervisor on duty that inmate Knight was heading back to my unit and I was to pat him down before he got to his cell. My partner at the time was away from the unit, which meant that I would have to call over to A unit and ask for assistance. I got my pal Mo on the phone, and told him my orders. All the while, Knight was banging on the unit door, insistent the officer in the bubble let him in.

Mo replied, "Don't you dare do anything 'til I get there."

I immediately hung up the phone and was heading out of the office when Knight was let into the unit. He headed up the stairs to his cell. I called out to him, "Knight, I want to see you in the office."

He ignored my order and proceeded to his cell. I let the bubble officer know that we were going on the range to pat down Knight.

Mo was just coming in the unit door and we marched up the stairs. At the top, we were met by inmate Chapple, who was deliberately blocking our way. I pushed Chapple against the bubble window, and told him to move aside.

As I tried to go past him, he attempted to trip me. I ignored him and was focused on heading down the range. Mo then stepped in front of him and kept Chapple against the bubble window. He told Chapple not to move, then followed me to the range.

We could hear Chapple yelling, "Williams, you're a goof. Who the fuck do you think you are?"

As we got to Knight's cell, he stepped out and said, "What's up?" He complied with my pat-down order, but since Chapple stalled us, we found nothing on Knight, and assumed he threw it out his cell window, which was open at the time.

We walked off the range and reached the common area, just outside the bubble. There we were met by seven or eight more inmates, including Chapple who again called me a goof and told me that I had no right to push people around.

A heated argument started, and we were soon rapidly surrounded by more inmates. Chapple and I were nose to nose, and his voice kept getting louder and louder. I looked to one side, seeing Mo had now turned his back to mine. We both realized that we were now surrounded by at least a dozen inmates.

The officer in the bubble had opened his gun port, but was not able to see us since inmates blocked his view.

Next Chapple sneered, "Fuck you, Williams!"

I said, "Fuck you, too."

Chapple responded in kind, but this time he took a step backwards. I responded in the same manner, and also took a step back, which put Mo and I closer to one another.

Chapple responded verbally again, and the next thing I knew Chapple turned and headed down to his range. The group of inmates that surrounded us slowly disbanded, which allowed Mo and I to exit the upper range and head to the living unit office. Once safely inside the office with the door locked, we took a big sigh of relief as we both knew that things could have gone badly for us.

Shortly thereafter, we returned to the range to conduct the lunch-hour count before inmates were let out for dinner. After my unit was locked up, Mo returned to his unit. Once the count was good, the bubble officer opened the units up, and the inmates exited to dinner.

Approximately five minutes later, Chapple came down from the upper range and stuck his head in the office door before heading out to the dining room and said, "Fuck, Cookie, that was a close one."

I responded, "Let's not do that again!"

He laughed and then left the unit for the dining room.

To this date, as luck would have it, we seemed to have a positive outcome. Such is prison culture.

RANDOM SEARCH

The next day, while conducting a random search of all the inmates coming out of B unit, myself and a supervisor escorted inmate Knight up to the health care unit and the supervisor proceeded to search him in the doorway of J and K units.

Knight looked at us both and did not resist. The supervisor took from inmate Knight one piece of wooden doweling, 16 inches in length by one inch by two inches, and half a pair of scissors (approximately 8 inches in length) that was tied to his wrist with a piece of torn cloth. Also removed from Knight was one Weider weight belt that was wrapped around his waist. Inmate Knight then was taken to J-unit segregation.

The reason for searching inmate Knight was the day shift supervisor had received information that Knight was going to stab another inmate in the gym during the population recreation time. Knight was charged and placed in segregation.

CHAPTER 6

TRANSFERRED TO
MOUNTAIN INSTITUTION

Mountain Institution central control.

In May 1990, I was successfully transferred to Mountain Medium Security Institution. Mountain was in 1962 a detention centre for the Sons of Freedom Doukhobors. It housed both male and female inmates and the buildings mostly consisted of dormitory-style metal huts with small living areas to discourage the traditional burning of buildings that characterized the Doukhobor method of protest.

In 1964, the female Doukhobor inmates were released and older non-Doukhobor male inmates were admitted, which changed the population dynamic. Many of these original buildings remained in use when I was at Mountain Institution, but now it had been modified to suit the needs of the newer style of institutions of today, including better security and placement of the buildings, with open-concept units and control posts located in the middle of the building giving correctional officers a better view all around.

I enjoyed working at Mountain. I spent six months as case management officer, where I would assist other correctional officers with their reports and ensure inmates on their caseloads were following their plan.

Mountain Institution was a far cry from Kent Institution. The inmates were more relaxed due to the fact that the majority of the population were protective custody inmates. The inmates were friendly to the point that it made me personally feel uncomfortable, which was probably due to my 13 years working in maximum security institutions. I was not used to such familiarity.

KENT INSTITUTION, HELICOPTER ESCAPE

June 18, 1990. On a nice sunny early summer day, I was working day shift at Mountain Institution. I and fellow officers were enjoying our morning coffee and a cigarette just outside the end of the south unit building in the main compound.

We were chatting away when all of a sudden in the distance we could hear what sounded like helicopter's blades thumping off the ground. My experience in the military, working near helicopters, told me that this particular helicopter was flying low to the ground.

We couldn't see the helicopter at the time from our vantage point, but knew it was in close proximity to Kent Institution. Shortly thereafter, we heard gunfire coming from the same direction.

I immediately ran to the front gate and informed the officers on post what we heard. Seeing that I had just recently transferred to Mountain, my first response was to go help my fellow officers at Kent, but when I reached the front gate I was told to report back to my post.

I found out later that a fellow officer with whom I had worked at Kent had been shot in the leg, although his injuries were not live threatening at the time. I felt sick to my stomach that one of our own had been badly hurt. It affects us all. We all wanted to be there for one another. It was one of those things that it could happen to anyone of us.

There were a number of reports as to why this escape was not successful, but what I found out later, shortly after the escape attempt was that it was originally a well-planned escape, and probably would have been successful with one small exception. The unexpected occurred.

Prior to the day of the escape, Kent Institution management team had decided to lock down the institution and conduct an institutional search. This usually means that the institution is shut down, and all the inmates would be sent to the outside exercise yard during this time. Ford was working in the industrial area of the institution, and this is where the helicopter was to pick him up, which threw a bit of a wrench into his plans.

When Ford found out about the institutional search, he somehow arranged to get a phone call out to attempt to have the escape cancelled; but unfortunately for him, the man responsible for commandeering the helicopter could not be reached and that part of the plan was already in play.

The second part of the plan included a float plane, which was to pick up inmate Ford on Harrison Lake and apparently take him to the USA. This part of the plan was cancelled after Ford's phone call.

Inmates Ford and Thomas were later recaptured by the RCMP swat team on Echo Island on Harrison Lake without incident.

LIVING A NIGHTMARE

Chilliwack Progress, February 27, 1991

By Robert Freeman

On June 18, 1990, a nightmare began for pilot Fred Fandrich of Valley Helicopters. The events of the day still haunt him now.

A man showed up at his Hope office wanting a helicopter ride — right into the yard of Kent prison where two cons waited to make a spectacular bid for freedomm [sic].

"Hey," the man said sharply, as Fandrich unlocked the office door at about 7:30 a.m. to get ready for an 8 a.m. flight.

Fandrich turned to see a man dressed in coveralls, a gas mask covering his face, and pointing a machine gun.

With the gun to his head, 51-year-old Fandrich was ordered by the nervous gunman to fly to the maximum security prison near Agassiz.

In the next hour, Fandrich had the dubious distinction of being an unwilling part of the first helicopter escape from a Canadian prison. However, for the cons, it was short-lived, as two inmates were arrested on an island in Harrison Lake only a few days later. A third man was also since been arrested and charged.

Not too surprisingly, the three-hour ordeal left Fandrich with a form of post-traumatic stress syndrome and nearly cost him his helicopter business.

After the escape, whenever someone tried to get Fandrich's attention by saying "hey" or "Fred" his knees would buckle and he'd drop limply to the ground.

"It's an emotional thing," Fandrich said in an interview last Friday. "I lost interest, particularly in my business."

"A half dozen times, I go out there (to the small Hope airstrip) alone and I see a vehicle, I go right on by."

One day while taking off in his helicopter, he saw a vehicle parked across the road that runs by the airstrip.

"I flew right over them, hovered right on top of them and reported the licence number to the police," he recalls.

The hardest thing for the 23-year veteran helicopter pilot was to fly again.

"What happens is your mind wanders and you relive parts of (the escape) — not the whole thing, just parts of it."

After therapy sessions for both Fandrich and his wife, Carol, he is flying more now and his interest in the business has returned.

A helicopter-golf venture he began two years ago is coming together with some backing from "a major Japanese firm" and the knee-buckling episodes have decreased.

Doctors told Fandrich to talk about the escape until he was sick of it, he has pretty much reached that point.

(The last prison official Fandrich saw was a stress counselor the day his abductors released him, and he was so stressed out at the time he can't recall much of the session.)

The abduction of her husband, and the possibility that it could happen again to any helicopter pilot, angers Carol Fandrich.

According to a confidential report by Corrections Canada, prison officials suspected a helicopter break out, but never warned any local helicopter pilots.

"I'm mostly angry that this sort of thing happened and (prison officials) aren't doing anything about it," she says. "It could happen to any pilot, anywhere near a prison."

No one from the prison has ever called Fandrich for his opinion on how to prevent helicopter escapes, nor has compensation been paid for the damages to his helicopter or for the business losses that resulted from his abduction.

One of the simplest ways to prevent helicopter escapes, Fandrich says, is to string quarter-inch cables across the prison yard.

While Corrections Canada develops a policy to safeguard prisons from helicopter escapes, Fandrich has taken his own security steps so that police will be notified should anyone try another escape with his helicopter.

One reason why he moved from Agassiz to Hope, Fandrich says, is because he feared just such an escape.

When that fear became a reality, there was not much he could do except follow orders. One of the first commands was to kill time.

The gunman was too early. He ordered Fandrich to set the chopper down in a clearing near Ruby Creek, between Hope and Agassiz, and to stop again at Silver Creek on the east side of Harrison Lake where a getaway vehicle had been hidden.

The gunman handed him a piece of yellow foolscap with a map of Kent drawn on it. An 'X' marked the spot where he was to land.

To this point, Fandrich didn't know who or what he was dealing with, whether he had a lunatic or a criminal on his hand, or both.

The plan was to set the chopper down inside the prison yard for a maximum of 10 seconds, but things started going wrong quickly.

A contraband search inside the prison had kept inmates away from the spot where Fandrich was to pick up two prisoners cleaning up garbage.

After a few seconds, Fandrich saw corrections officer Ripley Kirby drive up in a green truck and the gunman sitting in the back seat of the helicopter started firing.

Kirby returned fire and Fandrich lifted off until two inmates came running toward the helicopter and climbed aboard.

They flew to Silver Creek, on the east side of Harrison Lake, where Fandrich's abductors tied his hand together, tied his feet to the helicopter skids, and told him that someone would be along at about 5 p.m. who could free him.

"They were looking after my own welfare," Fandrich says. "They were happy to be out and didn't want to do me any harm."

But Fandrich managed to quickly free himself and get to a nearby road that led to a logging camp, where he radioed police. He could have flown out, Fandrich says, but his abductors had taken the helicopter's battery to start their getaway vehicle stashed in the bush.

Looking back, Fandrich says there was never a chance for him to escape, although while flying over Harrison Lake he could have tilted the doorless helicopter and dumped out his three abductors.

Fandrich says he feared that he would be charged with murder for such an act, given the ambiguities of the legal system.

But killing three people in cold blood might also have been too much for the mild-mannered pilot.

Carol says other helicopter pilots are "awed" by her husband's story, but Fandrich had his own ideas about heroics in such life-threatening situations.

"Don't be a hero; just shut your mouth and fly."

CHAPTER 7

ELBOW LAKE INSTITUTION

Elbow Lake was a quiet institution nestled in the mountains and it was known as one of the Lower Mainland's best kept secrets. Well, for a few years anyway; but as we know, things are always subject to change, given time.

My ex-wife, Joy, at the time had taken a position at Elbow Lake Institution as Chief of Personnel for Elbow Lake and Ferndale minimum security institution in Mission; she spoke very highly of her new job, as well as the institution itself; she said it was so relaxing, mostly due to the staff and where it was located.

She highly suggested that I apply for a transfer; she felt the change would do me good, after being locked up for the last 14-years. She believed I would be a great fit with the atmosphere and the outdoorsy-like setting.

A position opened up a few months later and I applied for a transfer; a day or two later, Joy called me and said that the warden wanted to interview me for the position.

I drove up to the institution the day of my interview; upon my arrival, I was very impressed with its location. As I crossed the bridge, a small creek ran through the institution, along the edge of the property. Surrounded by trees and mountains, it looked exactly like where I wanted to be.

I reported to the correctional duty office, introduced myself to an older officer behind the counter, and told him I was there for an interview. The warden at the time was Tom Crozier; rumours were he was by-the-book type of warden who expected a lot from his correctional officers.

The officer behind the desk pointed out the window and said, "The administration building is right next door." So I turned and left. I noticed that the buildings were actually trailers. Some appeared to be added on to but, overall, it had a comfortable look about it. I walked in the door and said "good morning" to a lady sitting at a desk behind the counter and told her that I was there to see the warden.

She said, "One minute," and then proceeded to walk down a hall. To my surprise, Joy returned. "Good morning, the warden will see you now." She escorted me down to the end of the hallway where the boardroom was. The warden was sitting, leaning back in his chair on the opposite side of the table when I came in. "Take a seat, John. Let's talk."

He mentioned during my interview that he was a little concerned about how I used my sick leave, as the institution had a small complement of correctional officers, covering off some shifts would require overtime, and I got that he was all about the budget.

I did my best to assure him, that given the chance, I would probably improve my on my sick leave usage.

He just looked at me and nodded. "And I have heard that you can be a bit of a rebel." He was concerned if I would be a good fit, but in the end he decided to give me a chance and would take me on secondment; which means if I didn't fit in, I would just go back to Mountain Institution.

During my three months, I never took any sick days, and Officer Anderson and I were instrumental in capturing an inmate, who was unlawfully at large at the time, when he came to visit another inmate at Elbow Lake during inmate visits.

Three months later, I was informed that my transfer was approved.

Elbow Lake was a minimum security institution located 140 kilometres east of Vancouver, BC, and located 3 kilometres from Morris Valley Road in Harrison Mills, BC. It was originally designed as 50-man forestry work camp in 1976. When I arrived at Elbow Lake, we only had approximately 50 inmates in camp.

It is not your average federal prison; no bars, no fences, and no razor wire. The standard security features of Kent and Mountain Institutions are cast aside in favour of "Out of Bounds" signs and check-in and check-out policies.

It was carved out of a mountainside accessible by the Harrison East Forest Service Road. There were five huts housing the inmates, a main kitchen, TV/pool room and weight room/admin/stores/forestry officer and hobby shop, and of course our security duty office. Officers were not required to wear a uniform and usually dressed in casual clothing suitable for the mountain conditions.

For me, at the beginning, it was a bit of a culture shock; but I adapted in a short period of time to the open environment, which was way better than being in a controlled environment.

The most difficult part that I found hard to adjust to was how the counts were conducted; you had to know every inmate by face.

INMATE OVERDOSE

My very first incident at Elbow Lake was during a graveyard shift. The staff complement was only two officers on duty during the midnight shift. One of us would be stationed in the office while the other conducted the counts and rounds. It was as usual a quiet night. I just finished the 03:00-hour count and learned we were missing one inmate out of Hut 5. I returned to the duty office to inform my partner, who was a well-seasoned officer of English descent and had mainly worked in medium and minimum security institutions. I found him to have a bit of a negative attitude, but since I was new to the institution, I learned a long time ago, sometimes it is best to just sit back and take it one day at a time.

I informed my partner that I was missing inmate Douglas from the count. Policy was at the time to redo the count, and physically identify each inmate by name. Once again, once the count was completed, there was still no sign of Douglas. Next was a complete check of all buildings to ensure he had not broken into any of them. All were secure, so I reported back to the office and informed my partner, who called the RCMP.

It was not common at the time to take a drive down the access road or up the forestry road that passes behind the institution, which also had a gate.

My partner argued with me, "We don't do that here." I asked why, but he couldn't really give me a reason, so I just grabbed the keys, handcuffs, and a baton-type flashlight and headed out the door, saying, "I will give you a radio check when I am on the access road." I called in to do a radio check with his response, "Don't be too long. The RCMP are on their way."

I drove down the access road, along Morris Valley Road, turning a hard right at the stop sign and up the logging road. There was a gate across the back of our property along with your typical CSC Institutional sign, stating "Elbow Lake Institution," right beside the gate.

Just across the road from the gate, I spot what looks like a body lying alongside the road. I radioed my partner and let him know that I thought I'd found Douglas. I then stepped out of the truck clearly seeing that it was Douglas, face down on the ground. I walked up to him. There was no movement, so I poked him with the end of my 18-inch flashlight, and could not see him breathing. I knelt down to check him for a pulse, when all of a sudden, he started gasping for air.

I jumped back, gripping my flashlight, and didn't know what to expect next. That was when I noticed the white foam around his mouth. It was 03:30 in the morning, absolutely pitch-black out and dead quiet. My first shift on the job, go figure!

I radioed my partner and said, "You should get out here and give me a hand to put him in the back of the Bronco. I believe he is overdosing."

His response to me was, "You're a big boy. Put him in the truck yourself."

I was a little pissed at his response, so I turned it around so that I could load him in the back of the Bronco and returned to camp and the duty office. The RCMP was just pulling up and as the officer was getting out of his cruiser, I informed him that I found our missing inmate on the logging road, passed out on the ground. He came over to take a look at Douglas and immediately he confirmed my suspicions. "You need to call an ambulance." I was to transfer Douglas into our security van and turn on the emergency lights and follow him.

He gave me a hand to move Douglas into the security van. We placed him on a blanket and off we went. I followed him with my lights flashing. We made record time, taking 30 minutes to meet the ambulance at the turn off at the Trans-Canada Highway. The ambulance attendants were awaiting our arrival and once we had him on the gurney and loaded, they assessed him and gave him a shot of NARCAN to quell the overdose. They were able to get him stable and then off to Chilliwack General Hospital Emergency.

I thanked the RCMP officer, who took my name for his report, and I was off, following the ambulance to the Chilliwack General Hospital. When I arrived, I phoned the institution and let my partner know that Douglas would be admitted for a few days to monitor him. And that I would probably need a relief. He informed me that he was on it.

It took four shots of NARCAN to bring Douglas back; he was awake when I left.

I asked him, "How the hell did you get out on the road in your condition?"

He said he "had no idea." The last thing he remembered was being in the park, sitting next to the campfire. I assumed later that the other inmates packed him out to the road and left him there so as not to bring attention to them.

Six months later, Douglas was released on day parole and within 24 hours he overdosed. "permanently."

I never forgot what my insensitive "partner" did during that situation. Over the course of my career I have worked with a lot of good and not so good officers, but we always had one another's backs. "That was the basic survival rule."

The majority of officers that I worked with over the years at Elbow Lake were well-seasoned officers. When I first started at Elbow Lake, a majority of them had not worked in any other institutions other than Elbow Lake. Those individuals were accustomed to doing things their way. Over the course of the following years, though, more and more officers who worked at Kent Institution would eventually transfer into Elbow Lake, changing the overall dynamitic of the institution.

ATTEMPTED DRUG IMPORT

It was a nice sunny morning, March 7, 1992. Officer Anderson and I were working day shift and were enjoying our morning coffee in the duty office when the morning civilian cook arrived in the duty office to sign in.

"Why are three blue towels laying alongside the access road," he asked.

Officer Anderson and I had no idea. "Where on the road did you see them?"

The cook said, "About 50 yards down the access road."

I grabbed the keys to our security vehicle and headed down the access road to check it out. Sure enough, just about where the cook reported seeing them, I found three blue towels lying alongside the road. I pulled over and walked over to where the towels were and, looking over the embankment, I could see someone dressed in institutional greens, wearing a black balaclava. He was crunched down against the bank of the road, trying not to be seen. I said, "What hell are you doing? Get your ass up here!"

He climbed up the embankment with a very large walking stick. I told him to leave it, which he dropped. Once on level road, I told him to remove the balaclava. He pulled it off, and to my surprise, I saw inmate Nolin.

Once inside the vehicle, we headed back to the duty officer and I escort him into the office where he was placed in a temporary holding cell. I updated Officer Anderson on what happened. And seeing that I left the towels where they were, I decided to go back down and see who showed up.

I grabbed a set of handcuffs and headed down on foot to where the towels were. Just before I get neared them, I heard a car coming up the gravel road. I immediately stepped off the road and into the tree line. I ducked down as not to be seen and heard the car pull up. The drive honked his horn once and I stood up. Just as he spotted that I was not who he expected, he took off speeding towards the Institution.

I thought, *Not smart.* There was only one way in and one way out. I radioed Officer Anderson and told him that there was a grey-coloured two door vehicle heading his way.

He immediately locked up the office jumped into the security vehicle and proceeded down the access road. In the meantime, the vehicle in question had turned around and was heading back in my direction.

It was then I spotted a large Ziploc bag in the middle of the road and picked it up. I saw the car coming straight at me. I picked up a nearby rock, positioning myself in the middle of the road. I stood there, rock in hand, waiting.

Once he saw me, he stopped and shut off his vehicle. As he did, my partner drove up behind him and stepped out of his vehicle. I ordered him to step out of his vehicle and Officer Anderson came up behind him, handcuffed him, and we returned to the duty office. Officer Anderson called the RCMP, let them know happened, and that we had a very large bag of marijuana in our possession. In the end, the suspect was charged with attempting to bring drugs into the institution.

Officer Anderson and I received a letter from the warden following this event.

RE: Events on the Weekend of 1992-03-07

I wish to commend you respecting your performance on the apprehension of attempted importation of drugs into the Elbow Lake environment and the capture of inmate Nolin outside the institutional boundaries.

You have provided a clear working definition for staff and inmates of what we hope to achieve with dynamic security as opposed to simple static security. Your contribution makes Elbow Lake Institution a more secure environment and does such to allay the fears and concerns in the community, which we are obliged to protect.

Thank you for your efforts.

Sincerely,

Tom Crozier

Warden

VISITOR AND CORRESPONDENCE OFFICER

While working at Elbow Lake Institution, I volunteered to take on the task of being the only visitor and correspondence officer in the institution. This entailed receiving and processing inmate visitor applications and approving and notifying the visitor once they were security cleared. These responsibilities did not fall under our current job description as a correctional officer. But seeing that I liked a challenge, I thought, *What the hell? Why not? I like breaking new ground.*

Letter from the Warden:

Visitor applications

1. I am responding to your memorandum of 1994.02.01. My written reply is a result of not knowing when we may next meet.

2. I should have ensured the notes from the Morning Meeting were more detailed. I would like for the visiting review process to remain as is, with one exception. The one exception is for the Deputy Warden to sign the letters to those who are denied visiting.

3. My understanding is that you consult with the Deputy Warden on those applications you are unsure about or you are recommending a denial of visiting. Given this process, the Deputy Warden is the person who is making the final decision. As such then he should also sign the letters of denial.

4. The letters approving visiting should be handled the way you are doing them now. In these cases, you are the decision maker. As such then you should sign the letters.

5. I have no difficulty in the way the process works. I like the way you consult with staff in arriving at your decisions/recommendations.

6. I did discuss this topic with the Regional Administrator Correctional programs at the Regional Headquarters. He thinks you are the only CO-II in Canada that has such a role and decision-making authority. John you are breaking new ground on delegated authority. Sorry, only recognition: No Additional Pay.

7. Please see me if we need to discuss further.

Doug Black
Warden

FOOD SERVICE COVERAGE

It was Jan 7, 1994, I reported for day shift, and just was about to pour myself a coffee when one of the inmates working in the kitchen came into the duty office to inform us that the food service officer had not arrived. This was normally unusual as most food service officers are in before we arrive, so my partner called the assistant warden to let him know. As it turned out there was no one to run the kitchen for the day, so seeing that we had four officers on duty at the time, I volunteered to run the kitchen until they found a relief.

A correctional officer working in the kitchen was something never heard of before; and it definitely was not in our job description, but I was after all qualified for the job. So I headed over the kitchen, found a cook's white coat, then checked out the menu for the day. It was pretty simple assignment. After all, the inmates working in the kitchen pretty much had things handled, so all I did basically was supervise, and ensure that the quality of food was exceptional, as always.

It was interesting to see the look on most of the institutional staff's face at lunch time, me behind the steam table, serving food.

As a result, I received the following memo from the assistant warden.

> Food service Coverage
>
> I would like to thank you for your cooperation in having CO-11 John Williams fill in as a "Food Service Officer," on 1994-01-07.
>
> Feedback received was positive and needless to say I appreciated the cooperation from John
>
> I have verbally thanked John, but please share this memo with him. I have placed this memo on John's personnel file.
>
> Steve Bonnet
>
> Assistant Warden
>
> Management Services
>
> Elbow Lake Institution

ELBOW LAKE'S FIRST MURDER

March 10, 1994, I had been filling the position of acting supervisor for three months. My replacement had just been recently transferred to Elbow Lake a week prior and I was walking her through the duties and procedures of the job, introducing her to the staff members. It was my last day as acting correctional supervisor, and like every morning Monday to Friday, I was attending the morning briefing, which consisted of the Warden and the Senior Managers.

At approximately 10:40, we were just about to close the meeting. There was a knock on the door, and then the door opened and Anna the secretary said, "Excuse me." She looked at me and said, "The duty office has been trying to get a hold of you on your radio. They think inmate Noade has been killed."

I immediately excused myself from the table and headed to the duty office, with my replacement on my heels. My long-time friend and co-worker, Mo, was on the duty office desk, which would best be described as the nerve centre for the institution. He informed me that Officers Larry and Smitty were up in Hut 5, and while conducting rounds, discovered Noade in his room. It appeared that he had been murdered.

I immediately grabbed the Polaroid camera and headed out the door to Hut 5. Upon my arrival, Smitty was standing outside the hut, appearing very pale.

I proceeded up the stairs and entered the hut. Noade's room was next to the outer exit door. His door was open, and I proceeded into the room. Officer Larry was standing at the base of Noade's bed. I observed that Noade's body was completely covered with a blue institutional blanket, and only his lower left forearm was exposed. Where his head was, the blanket was clearly saturated in blood. Larry looked at me and said, "I am not sure if he has a pulse or not. I think I am feeling my own."

So I stepped next to Noade's bed and grabbed his wrist to feel for a pulse. His skin was grey and clammy to the touch. Looking around the room, I could see blood splattered on the wall behind his bed as well as the ceiling, and down the wall at the base of his bed. It was apparent that he had been beaten with something.

I did not feel a pulse, so I turned and asked Larry and Smitty to secure the hut. as they left, I pulled back the blanket covering his head to take a peek, and found that he had been severely beaten around the forehead and his throat has been slit, pretty much from ear to ear. I replaced the blanket and proceeded to take numerous pictures of his room and the condition it was in.

I noticed that there was a full glass of orange juice on table next to his bed, and that it had not been disturbed. The room generally did not appear to be in disorder, so I assumed that he was sleeping at the time of his assault. I asked Smitty to secure Noade's door and remain outside until the RCMP arrives. I radioed Mo to get on the PA system and order all the inmates back to their units, and that we would have to utilize all the staff within the institution to confine the inmates in their huts. Later when the RCMP identification team arrived I escorted them up to Noade's room, I was standing in the door way, looking at the bloodstain pattern on his walls and ceiling, and I just mumbled out loud, "The assailant must have been left handed."

One of the RCMP officers looked up at me and said, "Yes, you're absolutely right, as if the assailant was right-handed the splat line would be across the ceiling in a 34-degree angle."

I informed them that I had taken pictures of the room prior to their arrival and handed over the photos that I took. I then returned to the duty office. The RCMP wanted to interview and strip search every inmate, and video tape each interview. I was assigned the task of running the video camera, and so for the next eight hours, every inmate was strip-searched, interviewed, and recorded. In the meantime, a search was conducted of Noade's unit, and Larry found something rather odd in the laundry room in the washer. He had found one set of jeans, one T-shirt, underwear, and a pair of socks in the washer with blood on them, so he placed them in an evidence bag.

At the end of the eight-hour interviews, we had no suspects. It was not until later that we learned, from an inmate source, who murdered Noade. A note was left in the inmates' outgoing mailbox, and read as follows:

Being an inmate at Elbow Lake Institution in the month of March of this year I have the following to say in regard to Jimmy Noade's death.

Mike Marshall and Mike Billingsley were on pills (valium) for a few days, I believe it started the day Jimmy went to outside court. We all knew each other since May of 1992 when we were in R.R.A.C in Matsqui Institution. Anyway, Jimmy went to outside court and the two Mike's starting doing pills they were all screwed up, when Jimmy came back from court he wasn't too happy at their action and cut them off their drugs and money source as they put out for Jimmy. They weren't' happy with that and started hanging around with each other leaving Jimmy alone, as that's the way he wanted it, he didn't want nothing to do with their pills and their punk action. On March 9th the two mikes were over at my cell and had eaten already about a dozen valium and sat and ate 8 more each at my place. They could hardly walk I told them to go home. The stopped off at another inmates house who wasn't home and poured shampoo on his pillow. The next morning mike Marshall came back to my house and just before he got here he was confronted by the inmate who's pillow got shampooed, mike told him to "Fuck Off," get your story straight, He then came to my house to ask if I had a joint. I told him no I didn't. He then told me that this inmate that just accused him of shampoo-ing his pillow better watch it, or he was going to get it. He then left and myself and another inmate went for a walk where we ran into the inmate that had his pillow shampooed, He told us that Mike Billingsley pulled a butter knife on him and another inmate told him t put it away. There were a few punches thrown and the inmate received some scars to various parts of his body.

He said they were crazy and they were going to kill him. I told him to stay with us and I would talk to them as I was their kitchen con-nection so we got them to leave Bruce alone. Mike Marshall asked me on that same morning if they went and robbed Daliwal would he "rat on them" I said yes he probably would, he replied we will wear balaclavas. I head through the prison grapevine that they did attempt something with Daliwal but he fought back so they left him alone. Mike Marshall told me in his house also that day we were being stripped searched and then had dinner in the kitchen. When I was in the kitchen I sat for a minute with Mike Billingsley, he asked me if it was me over looking for Jimmy earlier, I told him no. Upon talking to another inmate, he told me he went over there at 10:00 o'clock looking for Noade and Mike Marshall was blocking the entrance going into Hut 4. The inmate asked Mike if Jimmy was awake as he wanted to see him, Mike said No, he wasn't and to check back at noon. What got me is Mike Billingsley had to be in Noade's house to hear this inmate ask if Noade was awake, or he wouldn't of asked me cause he didn't know who it was. I know they killed Jimmy and I think they are bonders and will not sign my name as they will get out someday and I know they will be looking for me. By then I'll hopefully be 60 years old and ready to die because that's what they do. Noade was going to get it too if he didn't smarten up. I asked what he meant and he said he's being a "Cunt." I heard later that Noade called him a couple of punks and that they were cut off.

About two months ago I got a small knife from the kitchen to give them to cut up their tomatoes, roast beef on whatever, I brought them. The morning of March 10th the two mikes sat there having their breakfast and I went over to see if they needed anything. Mike Billingsley told me "We don't need fuck all." They seemed to be something wrong but I couldn't put my finger on it. I finished my job at 8:15 and went home where I started cleaning and redecorating my room around, when my neighbour came in around 10:15 or something and said they killed Jimmy, I replied yea right, he said I am serious they killed him, I knew right away who did it.

This is very scary writing this out in Jail, I've had 2 people walk right into my house since I've started, I was going to redo it to make it easy reading, but I have to live here. I hope you keep your word, I know how investigations go and if you're taking to the Mikes, and my name is mentioned you never know what can happen when you're in Jail.

Will consider testify but like I said I know these guys, they will get me, it make take awhile but I know they will.

This was the first murder at Elbow Lake work camp near Harrison Hot Springs. It shocked all the staff and inmates, who together chipped in $520.00 towards Noade's memorial service.

STABBING DEATH DRAWS MURDER CHARGES FOR TWO ELBOW LAKE PRISONERS

Chilliwack Progress, October 12, 1994

Two prisoners have been charged with second-degree murder in connection with the death of a fellow inmate at Elbow Lake institution last March

Agassiz RCMP say Michael Robert Billingsley, 24 and Michael Scott Marshall, 23, were charged with the murder of 25-year-old James Robert Noade, who was found beaten and stabbed in his cell bunk March 10.

At the time of his death, Noade had served 19 months of a three-year sentence for causing bodily harm with intent to endanger life.

Elbow Lake, a minimum-security federal prison, includes many prisoners transferred from higher-security federal prisons. Inmates, housed in individual rooms within large trailers, are able to lock their doors from the inside.

Billingsley and Marshall, both federal inmates, were charged Oct. 5 after an [sic] and are being held at a higher-security institution, where they were transferred immediately after Noade's murder. They are scheduled to appear in Chilliwack Provincial Court Oct. 14.

PRISONERS SENTENCED

Chilliwack Progress, April 12, 1995

Two Elbow Lake inmates charged with brutally beating and stabbing a fellow prisoner to death have been sentenced for manslaughter.

Michael Scott Marshall and Michael Robert Billingsley, both 24, were sentenced in Surrey Provincial Court Tuesday to extended jail terms.

Marshall received a seven-year jail term and Billingsley had a five-year sentence added to the time he's now serving.

Both were prohibited for life from possessing firearms or explosives.

Marshall and Billingsley were originally charged with second-degree murder after inmate James Noade was beaten and stabbed to death in his bunk March 19, 1993.

SWORN TO SECRECY, BUT STILL FRUSTRATED

Patricia Scott was an antiques dealer from south-east London. She replied to Kent Institution inmate Williams' advertisement for pen friends. She knew that he was serving a life sentence for the murder of a woman during a sex attack. But she told family and friends that he was reformed.

Patricia Scott was murdered while on an extended conjugal visit inside Kent Prison after marrying inmate Williams.

Williams poisoned her to inherit her money, and then he made it look like he had also overdosed; later he tried to explain that he had tried to kill himself as part of a suicide pact they had made.

Mrs. Williams' family had been concerned by the marriage. Her brother flew from London after receiving the news of his sister's death; he reached out to the community for support and received several letters from a few correctional officers.

Several officers contacted Matthew Plumtree of the *Chilliwack Times*. The following letter was sent to the *Chilliwack Times* in response to her murder.

> It has taken me a long time to write you, for fear of losing my job. I work for Corrections Canada as a guard. Your desire to hear from Corrections is commendable; however, the response is slim to nil.
>
> Please don't be disappointed. We as Peace Officers are sworn to secrecy, Should we speak up in regards to an issue and our names

are revealed, we have lost out jobs on that basis alone. I will help and assist you with whatever I possibly can as long as I have your re-assurance not to reveal your source.

The letter writer then explains how inmates, many of them, violent sex offenders or child molesters, snag their prey.

I have personally witnessed the direct and indirect contact child molesters have with children and the severe manipulation violent sex offenders use to catch their prey.

You see to these outcasts of society, these women are their ticket to release. If conditions are established for the offender to show their caseworker that "family" ties exist outside the institution, that gives the offender an extreme leverage tool to manipulate for Private Family Visits and an added advantage to access children.

The offender themselves tell the woman what they are in prison for and rest assured it is the "offenders version." He usually states he is innocent or that he was not his fault.

Due to the oath of secrecy their caseworkers are not obliged nor permitted to advise the female contacts of the prisoner's offence no matter how horrifying or violent, it may be. Prison guards, as myself, see this daily and would love nothing better than to have the opportunity to converse with these women, but again we are not permitted to do this. We complain bitterly that we are unable to protect the public; the very words printed in the correctional Mission Statement is to Protect Society.

I hope this letter assures you of the support and sympathy we guards share with you. The only consolation I can give you at this time is that we (the guards) do have our own discreet tactics to make life miserable for those guys on the inside and that there are times when we are able to seek revenge. When we do, we do it for you and your sister and Victims.

I was so personally offended by this officer's letter to the editor of the *Chilliwack Times*, and took it upon myself to write a rebuttal.

Dear Editor

I am writing you regarding an article published in your paper (April 29, 1994), titled Sworn to Secrecy, But Still Frustrated.

I have been a correctional officer for 18 years and after reading the letter, found myself rather upset. First off, let me say that I myself, as all prison staff across Canada, share great sympathy for the loss of Mr. Scott's sister. The loss of a loved one is never easy.

But my reason for writing is regard the "guard" who's letter you published April 29. I, as well as my fellow peace officers, do not want the general public thinking that all correctional officers think like this individual does.

The article states "we the guards have our own discreet tactics to make life miserable for those on the inside and there are times when we are able to seek revenge."

There is no collectivity of guards. Correctional Officers are individuals each with his own beliefs. We do not necessarily think alike. It is not our mission to judge and punish inmates. This had already been done by the court system. When correctional officers start thinking of themselves as judge and jury then they have lost insight into their job. This kind of thinking is archaic. It can endanger an officer and his peers, as well as the inmates.

We took an oath, not just to secrecy, but to uphold the law. Like our Fellow RCMP officers, ours is not an easy job. The judicial system is not perfect, but when we start thinking that we can act above the way by judging those already judged and sentenced then we are no better than vigilantes.

We may not all agree with some of the policies of corrections, but we have a job to do and I believe that, generally, correctional officers do the best they can with the policies given to them.

John Williams
Correctional Officer
Elbow Lake Institution.

As a result, my letter was published in the *Chilliwack Times*; however, when I returned to work the day after it was published, I was called into a meeting by senior management of my institution. They fully understood how I felt at the time but noted that I should have approached them first before responding to the article.

As a result of my actions, I was given a verbal warning and told not to do it again unless I consult with them first. "Noted."

HOSTAGE NEGOTIATOR TRAINING

May 06 to May 10, 1994

John Williams

Correctional Officer

Elbow Lake Institution

Dear Mr. Williams:

Congratulations on your success at the Hostage Negotiator Training session.

I understand you were one of only four staff members who received the designation of Primary Negotiator. Many staff does not achieve the primary level designation until the second time through the training.

Hopefully, we will never need to utilize your new talents at Elbow Lake Institution. However, your talents may be requested at another institution, as negotiators are sometimes needed at other sites for training and "for real."

I will see what I can do to have you included in one of the contingency training exercises during this fiscal year at either Kent or Mountain Institutions.

Your success on the training session is well deserved.

Yours Truly

Doug Black

Warden

I attended a training session at Kent maximum security institution once; it was a mock-up hostage situation. I arrived at Kent Institution after I got the call and reported directly to the warden's board room for the briefing.

The situation was the female schoolteacher who taught in the institutional school had been taken hostage; the offender was a long-time sexual offender serving 15 years for sexual abuse with a lengthy history of violence towards women.

I was teamed up with a relatively new correctional officer; he was young and ambitious and would be taking the primary negotiator position, which meant he would be the one in control of negotiations and would communicate directly with the offender. Once the briefing was over, we reported to our communication room, where he called the inmate on the speaker phone. The offender was actually a supervisor that I had worked with for a good many years, and he knew how to play a bad-ass offender. Communication started out with the basics: Is everyone alright? Etc. I started to realize at that point that this situation was not something we could negotiate. Due to his past criminal record and long history of violence towards women, it would be best to let the ERT take over. But he was determined that he could negotiate her release. The inmate went as far to say that he would seriously consider turning over the teacher if he was to come down to the school to meet face to face.

Well, we were trained not to go there, as it could create complications that could result in one or both—meaning the hostage and the hostage negotiator—getting hurt. But he was in charge, and off we went to the inmate school. Once we arrived, we were separated by a sliding barrier; the school door was some 29 feet away, and the inmate had the school teacher in front of him, with his arm around her neck, in his other hand he had what looked like a knife (which was actually rubber prop). The inmate said, "You need to come closer. I'll let her go once you do, and we can talk."

Well, the new correctional officer told the bubble officer to open the barrier, and he stepped through. The next thing you know, the inmate stabbed the school teacher, which by the way was a female correctional officer who was instrumental in training all hostage negotiators. He then threw her to the floor and lunged at my partner and stabbed (pretended) him aggressively.

It was an experience that I am sure my young partner will never forget, and a freshly planted reminder that we never meet face to face for that reason.

I remained a hostage negotiator for some six years after my original training, and actually only used it once in a real-life situation. I was coming out of a local store in Harrison Hot Springs one evening, when I noticed there was a police car just outside the door entrance. The officer was sitting in his vehicle with the window down, and I could hear him talking to his dispatcher. What caught my attention was that the dispatcher was informing him they had received a call from a woman who was going to commit suicide; she was at a local phone booth, but would not tell the dispatcher of her location. The officer asked for a hostage negotiator and was informed that one was not available at the time. I walked up to his car, and pulled out my correctional identification, and said, "I am qualified, if you would like my assistance."

In the end, I was able to talk to the woman over his radio, and was able to get her name, and her location. An ambulance was dispatched to her location within minutes and in the end, everything turned out okay. The skills that I did learn helped me throughout the years on the job, as well as when I took on the role of working in the union.

CHAPTER 8

FIRE FIGHTING

When I arrived at Elbow Lake in 1991, it was mainly a forestry work camp with a forestry fire fighting program. At the time it had a 20-man unit fire crew, which could be called out to forest fires in northern BC for a maximum of ten days and was escorted by two forestry officers. Each inmate would have to be eligible for day parole to be approved for the 20-man unit crew and had to have the necessary training.

There were also two 10-man contact crews, which could be called out to do local mop-up fires. Every inmate was required to have first aid as well as basic fire suppression and portable pump and water delivery training, which was conducted in the institution or at the Haig fire training school in Hope, BC.

UNIT CREW:

... specialize in larger fires and are used when fires grow beyond initial attack resources. Unit crews establish pump and hose lines, dig fire guards, burn off fuel from the fire's path, and use chainsaws to cut fuel breaks and remove danger trees. For wildfires in remote locations, or those which require a high level of response for an extended period of time, unit crew personnel may live in a temporary fire camp and work for 14 days in a row. (Province of British Columbia 2020)

CONTRACT CREW:

Once a fire, or area of a fire, is considered to be under control (i.e. contained) contract crews (Type 2 firefighters) may be utilized to; 'mop up' a fire using pumps and hose lays; to patrol areas in which a wildfire has burned using hand tools to extinguish any remaining smokes or hotspots; and, to complete the removal of equipment from fires once they are fully extinguished. (Province of British Columbia 2020)

When I transferred to Elbow Lake, no correctional officers volunteered to take out fire crews; it not something that officers wanted to do because it was not in their job description. But for me, I was never one to limit my abilities and I found myself attracted to the thought of fighting fires.

It would be a personal challenge, and something that I really wanted to experience firsthand; I enjoyed working with the inmates, and seeing that our job really did not offer any real job satisfaction, I sought it out in different areas, and fire fighting was something that I really wanted to do. So I contacted the warden to let him know of my interest; he was not bright on the idea at the time, but with my persistence, in time, he did come around, and correctional officers who wished to take the training would be considered to take out fire crews.

There were a few requirements that each of us needed, of course. For one, you had to have a class four licence that would allow you to operate vehicles: buses like trucks, called "crummys," which held a maximum of 12 people. (A crummy is a vehicle used to transport loggers or, in this case, fire fighter to the work site.) We also were required to have basic forest fire training. A few correctional officers, like me also received fire boss training, and I was the only correctional officer lucky enough to also receive the rapattack helicopter training in Abbotsford.

RAPATTACK CREW:

Sometimes wildfires will occur in areas that are difficult to access, either on foot or by vehicle and where there are no suitable landing areas for helicopters nearby. In these instances a rappel crew may be called on to respond to the fire. Firefighters rappel from a helicopter adjacent to the fire to take immediate action. Additionally rappel crews may be utilized to build helipads allowing helicopters to land and deliver personnel and equipment to difficult to access fires. (Province of British Columbia 2020)

West side Harrison Lake fire

My crew got called out on a fire that was just a few miles from our institution. It was in a logged-off area on the west side of Harrison Lake and had been caused by neglectful campers, who left a fire going on the edge of a landing. The wind had picked up and the wind blew the sparks into the tree line. We arrived and started to unload our equipment out of the crummy;

portable water pumps, hoses, shovels, chain saw and, of course, every fire fighter's trusty tool, a Pulaski, which is a special hand tool used in fighting fires—a combined ax and adze on a wooden handle.

The fire had swept up the hillside and into the timber line. Smoke erupted from the top of the hill, like a volcano.

One of the guys on my crew had fought fires before, so we were looking up the hill, trying to come up with a plan on how to contain it. There was a small creek running up the hillside that would give us the water we needed to run the pumps. We would have to establish a perimeter in order to stop it from spreading farther up the hillside. He would take four guys up the side with him and find a place on the creek where he could access water. Next, he would start to build a fire guard along the edge of the fire, so that it wouldn't creep underground.

They headed up the hillside and disappeared into the tree line that was covered in smoke. Twenty minutes later, the Chilliwack fire boss arrived. He informed me that they'd already had a spotter plane fly over the area and from what the pilot said, he had already called in a bomber to hit the top of the mountain to help contain it.

I looked at him and said, "How long do we have before it arrives?"

"Best guess, he said, "is 15 to 20 minutes."

"I have five guys on the side of the hill next to the creek setting up pumps and hoses." At that moment, we heard over the radio that the bomber was on its way; expected time of arrival was 15 minutes.

I looked at him and said, "I have to warn my guys," and off I went up the hill.

As I climbed up alongside of the creek, it seemed the smoke became thicker with every step. I could hear a chainsaw running a short distance away, and guys yelling back and forth to one another. I reached about halfway to the top, when I heard over my radio that the bomber was lining up on final approach, which meant that we were running out of time.

I could barely see through the smoke. When I spotted my guys, I yelled at them, "Stop doing whatever you're doing, and hit the ground. The bomber is on final approach and will be dropping close to us."

My crew gathered together and we lay face down on the ground, just as I heard the bomber fly overhead. The next thing we heard was the sound of crashing branches as the fire retardant hit the top of the trees.

It was over in seconds, I told the guys, "Leave everything where it is and head back down the mountain." We all got out safely and when we arrived back at the base of the mountain, the fire boss looked at me and said, "So that was a little too close for comfort," I looked at him and said, "That is an experience that I will never forget, never to be repeated again."

Luckily, we were able to contain the fine and get it under control after a Chilliwack 20-man unit crew arrived to assist us.

1994 Manning Park forest fire

MANNING PARK FOREST FIRE

We were called into assist with the mop-up on the Manning Park fire. When we arrived, it was something to see. It looked like a war zone, something you would see on TV. There were at least a dozen or more staging areas, and I counted eight helicopters at one time flying in and out, picking up equipment and crews. It was a big fire and had jumped from one mountain to another. It took five days of bombers and helicopters bucketing water during the day to get it contained. We were called in to knock down the hotspots.

When a fire was contained, forestry would fly over the fire areas and through thermal imaging they were able to see where there were still areas that were hidden under the debris and ash that needed to be extinguished. They would drop markers, which were very visual on the ground. We would be flown in by helicopter and then given a map as to where the hotspots were. Once we found them, I would call for a bladder of water and we would step up the pumps and extinguish them.

When we were all set up, we were then briefed by the forestry officer in charge, he notified us that he was going to assign us to work with a brand new 20-man crew from the Stó:lō Nation. They looked like they were just out of forest service graduation class—their coveralls were brand new and their equipment didn't have a scratch on any of it. Not like my crew, who looked like a ragtag mining crew, gruff and basically looking like a well-seasoned fire crew.

My guys teased the new Stó:lō crew, poking fun at them, about the way they looked, like they just got out of forestry school; it was all in good fun, and their way of welcoming them. We were assigned to a landing zone, where we would be flown by helicopter to the top of a mountain. Once we landed, we would split up into two teams and start searching for our hotspots. The day was going well, but later in the afternoon, the wind started to pick up, dark clouds began hovering over the mountaintops, and the wind became stronger. And then it was like night and day—the sun disappeared, and the wind started to gust.

We immediately packed up, as we were in the middle of completely burned out area where only black sticks resembled what were at one time full-grown trees. It gusted so hard that some of the standing dead trees started to fall into the mounds of ash that lay at their roots. Some of the trees were partly on fire on the inside, and as they hit the ground with such a thud that it sounded like a bomb going off, they exploded into fire once again. The tree line was some 150 yards away. I yelled over the radio, "Everyone into the tree line."

The wind was blowing so hard, it was picking up the ash on the ground and blowing it around, making it hard to see and breathe. We always worked in twos; it was safer that way. As we got into the tree line, I did a count, and was missing two of my guys. I got on the radio and confirmed that they were with the Stó:lō Nation fire crew. I told them to head back to our extract zone, as we were being called back. About 30 minutes later, we all met up at our extraction point, the wind was gusting pretty well, and I was a little concerned about a helicopter getting in to pick us up.

Just as I was thinking that, a yellow Bell helicopter came over the tree line, and tried to land. The wind was blowing pretty good at the time, so the pilot pulled up and tried it again. This time he landed with a thud as he hit the ground. He waved us in, and my guys loaded up as quickly as they could. We lifted off and by the time we got back to our loading zone, two of my crew was talking into a paper bags. It was a rough helicopter ride back to base, but we all made it back safe and sound.

Boston Bar Mountain fire

I was on vacation leave; I was sitting out on my boat, relaxing on Harrison Lake, enjoying the warmth of the sun and the peace and quiet of being out on the water. My cell phone rang. It was my supervisor from work. "What are you doing?"

I informed him that I was on my boat, he went on to inform me that the district forestry officer called and said that they had a fire and that they wanted me and my crew on it. I said, "Well, I'm on leave."

He said, "Well, it's up to you."

It took me about five seconds to decide, so I said, "Inform my crew to get prepped and I'll be in within the hour." Once I arrived at work, I was told that one of my guys on our crew was sick and could not make it, so the institutional forestry officer assigned me a recently new trained inmate. He was younger than most of the guys on my crew, and I was told that he was a good worker, but one with a bit of a youthful attitude. My crew had the crummy packed with equipment. I was given the directions from the district forestry officer and off we went. We arrived at our destination two hours later, to find a staging position all set up, along with a helicopter.

A staging site is where people, vehicles, and equipment are assembled for use. We pulled up, parked, and proceeded to meet with the forestry officer, who was standing next to his service truck. I had worked with this gentleman a time or two over the fire season; he was friendly individual, who had years of experience fighting forest fires. We shook hands and he said, "So, your boys ready for this?"

I responded, "They're a good crew of guys and hard working."

He then informed me that the fire we would be on was at the top of a mountain at the tree line. We would be flying up and dropping us off on the top of the mountain, and we would be assisted by a helicopter, which would be bringing in water with bladder bags. We were also be required to take a few small portable water pumps with us to mop up any hotspots.

So three of my guys loaded up a cargo net with the necessary equipment—pumps, water, lunches, shovels, etc.—that we required doing the task at hand. Everyone on my crew, with the exception of the new guy, had taken the training to work around helicopters. They loaded up the equipment and waited for the pilot to signal us to board. In the meantime, each one of us checked to ensure that our chin straps on our hard hats were fastened in place. If a hard hat ever came loose and hit one of the rotator blades of the helicopter, it could end in disaster.

I teamed the new guy up with a one of the other inmates who was well-seasoned and fire-trained; he was not happy that he was straddled with a rookie, but said he would take him under his wing.

The pilot signalled us to load, and bending over slightly, the first half of my crew loaded into the helicopter. I got in the passenger side and once strapped in, we were lifting off. We climbed up the side of a mountain. The pilot said, "I am going to drop your crew off on this rock cliff and then go back and get the rest of your crew."

In the meantime, I did not realize that the new guy had undone the strap on his hard hat. Up until this point, he had been following direction. When we landed on the rock face edge, I looked down, and the pilot was actually balancing the helicopter struts on the rock face, with the helicopter blades just about five feet from solid rock.

We exited the helicopter one at a time, with the new guy being the second person out the door. As he exited the helicopter, his hard hat lifted off his head and, due to the wind from the helicopter blades, bounced off the side of the door and down the sheer rock face, bouncing all the way to the bottom of the mountain. The look on his face was one of complete shock. He made his way along the rock cliff to the tree line, followed by the seasoned fire fighter that I teamed him up with.

The pilot looked at me, but did not say I word, I just sighed and then exited the helicopter as the last of the guys made their way to the tree line. When I arrived, I noticed the new guy standing with his back to me, holding his face. I said, "What's wrong?"

He turned around and looked at me, dropping his hands away from his face; I could see that he was covering up a new blackened eye. He said nothing about what happened, and I really didn't need to ask. He could have gotten us all killed, and he knew it.

As it turned out, he remained on my crew, for the remainder of summer season, and at the end of the season he turned out to be one of the best workers on my crew. We spent five days mopping up that fire, which was caused by lightning strikes.

On the last day, as the helicopter took the first crew off the mountain, I sensed that something was wrong. As the helicopter pulled away from the rock edge, it dipped sideways. When it turned, I saw red fluid running out of the back engine cover. The next thing I could hear was the helicopter pilot saying over the radio, "I've got a hydraulic leak and am going to have to do an emergency landing."

The helicopter engine howled as it descended the mountain. Then everything went quiet. Finally, there was a crackle over the radio. He was down and everyone was okay. Four of us had to wait for almost three hours until another helicopter could come and pick us up, but it was a nice, warm sunny day, and we did after all have a great view off the top of the mountain that we were on.

The fire fighting program was one of the best programs Elbow Lake ever had; although it was hard, dirty, physical work, it enabled the inmates to earn some money prior to release, and taught them how to work as a team as well as gave them a sense of pride.

Myself

ELBOW LAKE ESCAPEES SOUGHT IN MURDER

Although Elbow Lake had its fair share of walkaways, it really doesn't change the fact that most of the inmates that we were dealing with at the time were at one point from higher-security institutions. You can put all the safety precautions in place, but eventually some of them will walk away.

In 1999, Elbow Lake had 11 escapes, although most of them were eventually found within days of their escape and returned to custody, and most were usually picked up without any incidents to the general public. But unfortunately, there were exceptions.

In April 1999, two high-profile inmates walked away from Elbow Lake. There was a Canada-wide warrant out for their arrest in the connection with two deaths in Maple Ridge, BC.

ELBOW LAKE ESCAPEES SOUGHT IN MURDER OF CHILLIWACK MAN

Chilliwack Progress, May 4, 1999

By Mark Falkenberg

A Chilliwack man was one of two victims in a double murder being blamed on a pair of escaped inmates from Elbow Lake Institution near Agassiz.

Acting on a tip from a friend of the victims, Ridge Meadows RCMP discovered the body of Louis Maurice Croteau, 32, Thursday afternoon at a rural property in the community of Ruskin near Mission.

Yesterday police confirmed they found another body Saturday afternoon on the same property at 27855 96th Avenue, but did not release the identity of the 34-year-old second victim.

Police say their suspected killers, John Wonnacott, 51, a crossdresser with a three-decade criminal record, and convicted murderer Darby Cairns, 39, are armed and extremely dangerous.

On Monday, RCMP launched a massive manhunt for the two men, who walked away from the unfenced minimum-security Elbow Lake Institution on April 22.

Cairns had served exactly 14 years of a life sentence for first-degree murder, robbery and fraud when he went missing. He's described as 185 centimeters tall and weighs 86 kilograms, with a fair complexion, blue eyes, brown hair kept in1 [sic] a ponytail and a beard.

He has a burn scar on his right forearm.

Wonnacott, 51, was serving a combined sentence of 35 years and eight months for an on-again, off-again string of crimes that began in July 1968. His offences include robbery, aggravated assault, possession of stolen property, break and enter and theft.

He is described as 183 cm tall and weighs 73 kg, with a fair complexion, blue eyes and brown hair. He has tattoos and slash marks on his left arm. Police say he's known to dress up as a female.

Constable Dan Herbranson told reporters at the murder scene yesterday that Louis Croteau and the other victim knew the suspects, and that both victims were known to police.

WONNACOTT CAPTURED

Chilliwack Progress, May 14, 1999

One of the two Elbow Lake escapees suspected of killing a Chilliwack man in a double murder near Mission has been captured in Vancouver.

Vancouver Police arrested 51-year-old John Wonnacott outside the Dobson Hotel on Hastings Street about 9 p.m. Wednesday.

The cross-dressing Wonnacott, who has a criminal record stretching back three decades, was taken into custody without incident and was slated to appear in court in Maple Ridge yesterday to face charges of escaping lawful custody and being unlawfully at large.

He has not been charged in connection to the murder of Chilliwack resident Louis Croteau, 32, and Richard Thomas Hallett, 34, whose bodies were found April 29 and May 1 on a rural property in Ruskin.

Wonnacott walked away from the minimum security Elbow Lake Institution April 22 with convicted killer Darby Cairns, 39, who is still at large and is also being sought in connection with the Ruskin murders.

SECOND MURDER SUSPECT ARRESTED

Chilliwack Progress, May 18, 1999

By Mark Falkenberg

The second of two fugitives suspected of a double murder near Mission has been captured at a Vancouver rooming house.

Acting on a Crimestoppers tip, heavily armed police took convicted killer Darby Cairns into custody about 3:30 p.m. in the Chelsea Inn Rooms at 33 West Hastings.

"Our (Emergency Response Team) members surrounded the building; They went into the suite and arrested Mr. Cairns' without incident," says Vancouver Police spokeswoman Constable Anne Drennan.

"There were also two other men in the room; They could be facing charges of harboring a fugitive, but that hasn't been confirmed yet."

Cairns, 39, walked away from the minimum security Elbow Lake Institution April 22 with career criminal John Wonnacott, 51. Both men are suspects in the murders of Chilliwack resident Louis Crouteau, 32, and Richard Thomas Hallett, 34, whose bodies were found April 29 and May 1 on a rural property in the community of Ruskin in Maple Ridge.

Cairns' arrest came two days after Vancouver Police arrested Wonnacott at another Hastings Street Hotel in the same skid-row section of downtown.

Vancouver Police have sent Cairns back into the custody of Ridge Meadows RCMP. He and Wonnacott both face charges of escaping lawful custody and being unlawfully at large, but have not been charged in connection with the murders.

MY FIRST DUMMY

It was May 30, 2000. I was on graveyard shift. My partner and I were conducting the 0300 hour count through the units. My partner was doing one side of the hut, checking to see that every inmate was in his room, live and breathing, when he said, "I can't see this guy breathing." So I shone my flashlight on the ceiling of his room, which allowed me to see him more clearly. I couldn't see him breathing either, so I quietly unlocked his door and walked into his room, I tapped the edge of his bed with my foot, as sometimes inmates just react differently when they are woken suddenly. I have had inmates just jump right out of the bed.

Nothing happened, so I poked what appeared to me to be a body in the bed. Again, nothing happened, so I pulled back the blankets, and lo and behold, we found a dummy. It was my first dummy in 23 years of being in the service.

ELBOW HAS FIRST ESCAPE OF THE YEAR

Chilliwack Progress, May 30, 2000

A 26-year-old inmate who walked away from minimum security Elbow Institution last Tuesday turned himself in to authorities less than 24 hours later.

Daniel Brown was discovered missing by staff at the 3:15 a.m. inmate count, said Steve Bonnett, prison spokesperson.

"The unusual aspect of this was that the individual left a dummy in his bed dressed in bedclothes," he said. "Staff members are trained to look for inmates' breathing. The corrections officer said he saw no movement in the room."

Mr. Brown was serving a 10-year sentence for offences ranging from theft, B&E, and robbery, as well as obstructing an officer, failing to attend court, mischief, possession of narcotics and more.

He turned himself in by calling Elbow Institution from Mission and arrangements were made to have him picked up by Correctional Service staff and transferred to a higher-security institution.

This was the first escape of the year for the Harrison Mills institution. There were five walkaways in 1999, confirmed Mr. Bonnett.

CHAPTER 9

SO LONG ELBOW LAKE, WELCOME KWÌKWÈXWELHP HEALING VILLAGE

Elbow Lake had seen its time, much like many outdated institutions, so in 2001, it was transformed into a Native healing lodge and named Kwìkwèxwelhp Healing Village. The name Kwìkwèxwelhp is a Chehalis word meaning "a place where we gather medicine."

The powers to be realized in the early 1980s that there were a there were too many Aboriginal people in prison, and that a facility that offered Native spiritual need and programming was very much needed at the time.

The first step was to erect a long house; this would be the centre of learning and healing for natives, and non-Native offenders who follow the red path. Every morning we would attend morning prayers by the institutional elder.

Once the long house was finished, the building was blessed at the grand opening, which was attended by about 200 people.

It was the first in the Pacific region of its kind, and the first step in working together with first nation's offenders, the count at the time was 43, which consisted mostly of Native offenders.

It would be a learning experience for most of the non-Native correctional officer, as to the traditions of the First Nations people. As I have said before, changes don't come easy to those of us who grew up with old-school learning. But, in time, everyone got on board, and it was the best experience of my life.

I was one of the first correctional officers to do sweats with the inmates at Kwìkwèxwelhp Healing Village. As it turned out, the elder who held the sweats actually knew my uncle Raymond from working on the docks in Vancouver as a longshoreman. During one of the sweats that I attended, I was given a drum by one of the inmates who was on my caseload, and I still have it to this day.

We are not allowed to take gifts from inmates, but there was an exception given this time, as there was no hidden agenda, as it was an honoured tradition.

BLESSING THE LONGHOUSE

The Chilliwack Progress, October 28, 2001

By Shaw Hall

A traditional longhouse that will become a hub of learning and healing for natives in prison was blessed in a day-long ceremony recently.

The Elbow Lake Institution near Harrison Mills was re-named *Kwikwexwelhp*, a Chehalis word meaning "a place where we gather medicine," during the opening of the traditional longhouse, attended by about 200 people including natives, corrections officials, and elected officials.

The building was blessed in a sacred Chehalis ceremony rarely seen by anyone outside of the First Nation — involving a dozen dancers outfitted in rich costumes and elaborate masks.

"It was a historical event," said Jill Hummerstone, with Correctional Service of Canada.

"There has never been a longhouse-type building in a correctional facility anywhere in Canada. The teachings of the longhouse are utilized for the purpose of healing."

The longhouse is just the first step. The facility is being converted to an aboriginal healing village that will eventually be run by natives. It currently houses 43 offenders, most of them native.

"Now they have a place they can heal and reflect and gather," Chehalis chief Alexander Paul said after the blessing. "The long-house, this is our way. That's what's missing with our people."

Mr. Paul said many native people are lost, and he hopes the house will give offenders a chance to heal through finding pride in their heritage.

He said programs addressing basic reading and writing, substance abuse, physical abuse, life skills, and teaching native traditions will be offered.

Exactly what programs will be offered and how Corrections will recognize native ways are still being worked out.

Hummerstone said the longhouse represents two peoples coming together — the Chehalis and Corrections — but acknowledged there's still a lot of work to do.

"It's an education process, partly, and it's also one of partnership and inclusiveness. What's important is for us to be inclusive with Aboriginal people, to help them deal with their own issues. We've tried to cure Aboriginal people for many years, our new approach is that we're helping them help themselves,"

Judy Croft, director of the institution, said Corrections officials are working with a senate of Native elders and chiefs from around the Lower Mainland to determine the shape of the new healing village, and will then redevelop it.

The first step towards the longhouse was taken in early 1990s, when the Canadian government passes legislation stating too may Aboriginal people were in prison and encouraging facilities run by Aboriginal groups be established to help address the problem.

In 1997, the local Corrections commissioner and Chehalis agreed to work towards establishing such a facility at Elbow Lake, and in May commissioner Lucie McClung and Chief Paul signed a memorandum of understanding.

2000 DEATH BY NATURAL CAUSES

Officer Anderson and I were working day shift on the weekend. The two of us had worked together since the BC Penitentiary as well as Kent Institution; he was an exceptional correctional officer, and someone with whom I really enjoyed working. He was a soft-spoken gentleman, who kept to his traditional Christian beliefs, and had witnessed his fair share of institutional life. There were three of us working that day, along with a correctional supervisor. We were all sitting around chatting in the duty office when an inmate came running into the office to tell us that inmate Jakes had passed out in the weight room.

Officer Anderson and I each grabbed a portable radio and headed out the door to the weight room. Once we arrived, I noticed that Jakes was lying on the floor next to the bench press, which he had obviously been using at the time. I knelt down next to him, to give him a shake. Then he started to breathe funny. He rolled his head over as if to look at me, and I saw a tear build up in his eyes, and then it hit me. He had stopped breathing. I looked up at Officer Anderson and said "Call the supervisor. I think he's having a heart attack." I knelt beside Jakes, and tried to get a pulse; there was none. I said, "I'm starting CPR." As I started to do chest compressions, other inmates came into the weight room to see what all the fuss was about.

A number of the inmates had just taken the industrial first aid training that the institution had been offering at the time. I worked on Jakes for as long as I could and then Officer Anderson took over. I looked at the inmates and said, "Okay, who has first aid? Step up. Someone needs to assist Officer Anderson." A young offender stepped right up and knelt next to Jakes, then two other inmates took over, and we continued this until the ambulance arrived. Jakes was placed on a gurney and transported to Chilliwack General Hospital. We learned later that day that he died of a massive heart attack, and there was nothing that we could have done.

Jakes was a pleasant older gentleman, who was serving five years for drunk and driving charges. He had only been at the institution for about six months, was recently approved for private family visits, and had one coming up in a few days. I remember talking to him a day prior; he was excited and looked forward to spending a weekend with his wife of some 40 years. Of all the things that I have seen in corrections, his death was one that I couldn't block from my mind. Probably because I made it a habit not to look into the eyes of the dead. To me, it got personal when you did. But when I saw the tears pooling in his eyes, I swear I could sense the life flowing out of him at that very moment, something that I will never forget.

Officer Anderson and I received the following letter from the warden.

SUDDEN DEATH OF AN INMATE

> I want to recognize your professional response to a medical emergency involving an inmate at Elbow Lake Institution. Your diligence demonstrated a level of care towards others in terms of dealing with the medical emergency and the emotional well being of several men in the population who were traumatized by this event.
>
> Your commitment to the health and safety of Elbow Lake community is most appreciated.
>
> *Dianne Brown*
>
> Warden

INMATE ESCORTS

One of the responsibilities that we had as a correctional officers was escort duty, and at each security level there are many different types of escorts from medical, personal, and programs, to religious, just to name a few. In regard to maximum security inmates, they were always two officers on one inmate escort and were usually for medical or humanitarian reasons. They were, however, not armed during my first few years in the service. But that all changed when our new union UCCO-SACC-CSN was established.

Escorts could take just a few hours to a few days, depending on the reason for the escort.

One particular escort I was on is one that I will never forget. I was working with a fellow correctional officer, Fred, who was of First Nations descent and one of the best officers that I had the pleasure to work with during my years working at the Kwìkwèxwelhp Healing Village. He was a positive individual, and always had a great sense of humour. We were assigned to escorts that particular week, and we were asked by management if we would be interested in taking an inmate on a three-day escort temporary pass. The details were simple; we would be escorting a Native offender as well as one of the institutional elders, George.

We were to escort inmate Randy, along with George the elder, to his reserve in northern Manitoba to attend the funeral of his mother. The escort was for two nights, thus three days. We would fly out of Abbotsford into Winnipeg, and then we would have to catch a twin-engine turboprop plane the rest of the way to a little community near Randy's reservation and home. When we landed, we were met by the car rental company, who supplied us with a car that actually looked like an unmarked police car. We were also met by the local RCMP, who was there to escort us to the local detachment where we would lock Randy up during the evenings.

We arrived at the RCMP centre, and the officers were helpful and explained how the lock up procedure would apply to their detachment. They also supplied us with a local RCMP handheld radio and said our call sign would be *BC escort team*. As there was no cell phone service in the area, they had to rely on strictly radio communication.

They also gave us a map of the area, and seeing that where we were was pretty remote, there were not a lot of roads to get lost on. They said that the reserve had a First Nations officer, named Don, who would like us to report to him directly upon our arrival on the reserve.

So with George and Randy in the back of the car, and Fred at the wheel, we proceeded to drive out to the reserve to meet up with Don. A few hours later, we located the reserve, and the inmate actually directed us to where the First Nations officer's office was. We pulled up out front and standing on the porch was who I assumed was Don. He was a short stocky man, dressed in

RCMP uniform pants and a tan uniform shirt and dark blue jacket, pretty much like a RCMP work uniform.

He smiled as we exited the car, and said, "Welcome, come on in." We entered what I assumed was his own personal residence, as it had all the comforts of a home. He motioned us to have a seat at the kitchen table, and offered us coffee, which I was in dire need of. We thanked him as he proceeded to the kitchen to put get some cups, etc. When he returned with four cups of coffee, he placed them on the table and then sat down in a chair across from Randy. He asked Randy how he was doing, and said that was sorry to hear about the loss of his grandmother. It was obvious that Randy and Don had gotten along in the past when Randy was living on the reserve, so Randy thanked him and reached out to shake his hand.

Don then turned his attention to Fred and George, and asked them, "How was the flight out?" They responded and then he looked at me and started to make a joke about me being the only white man on the reserve, and that I would have to watch my back. At first, I didn't know how to take what he said, and was unsure if it was his upfront sense of humour or was he actually serious.

All that came to rest when he started to laugh under his breath after he had said it. A sigh of relief came over me, and from that point on we both threw jokes at one another, which usually ended in us laughing together.

He then explained that the ceremony would be in the lodge, and we were more than welcome to attend the dinner that evening along with traditional prayers. I stated that Randy understood that he would have to remain within sight and sound of Fred, I, or George at all times, and that he would be placed in RCMP lock up during the hours of 2300 to 0800. We would pick him up in the morning, head off to breakfast at the local restaurant in town, and then proceed to the cemetery burial service that day at a local church. We chatted for a few hours about this and then, noting the time, suggested that we head over to the longhouse for dinner.

We headed back to our respective vehicles and then proceeded over to the long house with Don leading the way.

The best way I could describe most longhouses is they are generally a large building made out of wood which sit about 100 or so people. The only opening in the whole building, other than the occasional small exit door, is the entrance door usually with a hole in the roof to allow for wood smoke to escape. Many of the longhouses I have been in have wood burning stoves for cold evenings. The front of the longhouse is often elaborately decorated with murals, numerous drawings, and the faces of heraldic crest icons of raven, eagle, bear, and killer whale. Longhouses are usually accompanied by a totem pole, situated just outside, with styles varied from one to another. Most longhouses have a kitchen and are best described as an indoor arena used for ceremonies, political meetings, various community gatherings, and spiritual events, such as the one we were attending.

We walked into the longhouse, which was dimly light with a strong wood smoke odour. There were four tables laid out on the floor of one end of the building, topped with assorted dishes of wild meat, fish, and various other dishes the locals brought with them.

We worked our way up onto the centre of the bleachers, so we would have a great view of the entire hall. The chief walked out to the middle of the floor, accompanied by a drummer, who solemnly hit his drum three times. The chief welcomed everyone, opening the event with a prayer.

There were dancers dressed in various coloured outfits, as well as drummers in one corner of the lodge. The drummers started to beat on their drums, along with a Native chant as the dancers danced around the circle floor in various moves as they yelped on occasion. I had no idea or understanding about Native culture, but in the years to follow, I would learn a great deal about Native traditions, past and present. My first sweat lodge experience was intriguing and spiritual, and would remain with me for years to come.

The evening went over as well as we expected. Randy was always within Fred's and my vision; when the evening ended, we proceeded back to the RCMP detachment to lock him up and return to our hotel.

The next morning, we picked Randy up at 0800, and proceeded to the local restaurant for breakfast. Once this was done, we drove over to where we thought the church was for the burial. The church was located on a small road in the local community not far from the RCMP detachment. We parked off the main road in hopes to catch the burial procession pass us by. What we didn't realize at the time was that the house that we were parked across from housed a local gang affiliated with a well-known high-profile motorcycle club.

The three of us were sitting in the car with the portable radio sitting on the dashboard of the car, listening to the occasional RCMP radio conversations.

I noticed a pickup truck pull out of the driveway of the house and drive in our direction. It then pulled up right in front of our car and as it was stopping, I noticed in the side mirror another vehicle pulling up behind us. It stopped and I watched the passenger door opening. Someone stepped out behind the door, but did not proceed any farther.

That was when Fred looked over at me and we both wondered what this was all about. We didn't think getting out of the car would be a good idea right then because we seemed to be cornered and were cautiously aware of the situation.

A rather large man stepped out of the truck in front of us and I noticed a passenger, who also opened his door but remained in the vehicle. He approached Red's side of the vehicle and started going off about staking out his home and what were we doing. As he was ending his questioning, the RCMP radio went off about the dispatch was requesting a PC (police car) to investigate a complaint received from a local resident who reported a white car parked out front of his house with three people in it and found it suspicious. And I can tell you I was really sure that if that radio call had not gone out, things could have gone very badly for Fred and I.

As the radio transmission ended, he stopped talking for a few seconds, stepped back from our vehicle, and took a serious look at the both of us and Randy, who was sitting in the back seat. He then suggested that we leave the area immediately. Fred and I looked at one another, and knew we had to get out of there while the getting was good.

We acknowledged what he was saying, and then Fred started up the car. As the large man was proceeding back to his pickup, he turned and signalled with the wave of his hand to the vehicle behind us to leave. Once both vehicles had backed away from us, Fred pulled out onto the street and said, "Now what do we do?"

I replied. "I think we should head back to the RCMP detachment and let them know what just happened since it was us that the complaint was about."

Once we arrive at the detachment, the three of us walked in and was met by the corporal on duty; he was smiling at us and then said, "What the hell were you thinking?"

Fred and I just looked at him and said, "We had no idea what was going on until the vehicles approached us."

Well, consider yourselves very lucky," he said. "That house has been on number one on our top-five list of gang-related incidents in the area, and they're not anyone to fool with."

In the end, we got Randy to his grandmother's burial, and this time we were escorted by an RCMP officer in a marked car.

We returned to our institution the next day with a wild story that I'm sure most of our fellow officers thought we made up. But Fred and I knew someone was looking over us that day, and we never forgot what happened, and how close things could have gone differently.

CLOSE CALL

Most escorts are usually one on one; this time I was taking an offender, who I will call Scott, into Vancouver to visit his sister, who resided in Vancouver in the low-rent district. We arrived on time, and I told Scott that he was to stay within sight and sound of me at all times. He looked over at me and said, "What if I have to go to the washroom?"

I just laughed and said, "Well, I will make an exception." We headed into her building and then entered the elevator to her floor. As we exited the elevator, I noticed three young Native brothers hanging out at the end of the hall. they paid little attention as we walked up to Scott's sister's apartment door. He knocked three times on the door. It opened, and I said, "Hi." She motioned us to come on in.

The apartment was small—one bedroom, with a living room that looked out at another apartment building. It was relatively clean, other than the fact that it was decorated with old-looking furniture, which looked well used. I couldn't help but notice the pleasant scent of cooking lingering in the air.

She walked up to her bother and gave him a hug and said. "Please have a seat. Would you like a cup of coffee?" I responded, and she was off to the kitchen. We sat around for what seemed a long time, but this happens on these types of escorts; we are after all the third wheel. Some escorts are a lot of fun to do, especially when the family makes you feel at home and includes you in the conversations.

We had dinner, which was wild game stew and freshly baked biscuits, which I gathered was what I had smelled when I walked in. The stew was outstanding, I enjoyed every bowl. She removed the dishes and we returned to the living room. Just I sat down, there was a knock at the door.

Scott's sister went to answer it, and I could hear a male voice saying, "Is he here?"

Next thing I knew, there were three men standing at the edge of the living room—the three that I'd seen standing at the end of the hall. They abruptly came into the living room. Two of them just flopped themselves down on the couch and made themselves at home. The third one stood at the edge of the living room, leaning against the wall with his arms crossed. Well, my bells and whistles started to go off; the one leaning against the wall was looking at me as if I was the enemy. I was thinking that probably most of them had done time themselves at some point.

The longer you work in prisons, you can't help but develop a sixth sense, and when you walk into a situation, you sense the atmosphere around you. I had at this time been in the service for some 25 years, and my bells were ringing like cathedral bells.

The one closest to Scott started to ask him how he was doing, and if the pigs were treating him properly, Scott said, "Yes, it's a pretty nice place to do time." He looked over at me, but didn't say a word. Then he looked at the guy standing against the wall and said, "Did you bring the beer in with you?"

"Yep, it's in the kitchen." He then turned and headed into the kitchen. I knew this was not going to end well and was thinking of ways to get us out of there without incident. That's when Scott looked at me and said, "I have to take a piss." I noticed that he ever so slightly winked at me. Then rose from the couch and headed off to the washroom, which was right next to the apartment door.

I waited until Scott was out of sight, and then stood up and worked my way towards the hallway as buddy was busy getting beers in the kitchen. I had no idea what was going to happen next, so I just put one foot in front of the other. The other two were chatting it up with Scott's sister. I actually think she knew what was going on, and kept the conversation going. As I passed by her, she looked up at me and I could see a look in her eye that said, "Get the hell out of here."

I was halfway down the hallway when I took my first breath. Scott was standing just around the corner. When he saw me, he turned and opened the apartment door, and I was right on his heels.

We got out to the hallways and instead of taking the elevator, we decided it would be faster if we took the stairs. We got to the main lobby and were out the front doors before they knew what happened. As we were getting into the institutional vehicle, I could hear them yelling from the balcony, "Hey, where you going, asshole?"

We got into the vehicle and were headed down the road when Scott looked over at me and said, "Fuck, that could have gone badly."

I totally agreed and thanked him for thinking on his feet. Years later, Scott was released, and up until point we always had a respectful relationship and joked about our experience until the day that he was released.

ROOFER

Prior to me working at the BC Penitentiary, I was working for a roofing company that was a privately owned three-man operation; I got the job through a friend in school who knew the owner. I was not big on roofing. It was a dirty job, but I found out the foreman that I was working for had done a little time in the provincial system. He was about eight years older than me, tall, long blond hair, and in really good physical shape. I only worked for him for about four months, before the owner ran the business into debt and had to shut down.

Some 17 years later, I returned to work after been off for four days on night shift and found myself on evening escorts. Seeing that we were a minimum security institution, correctional officers never wore a uniform; however, the inmates were required to wear work greens during the work day, but were allowed to wear civilian clothing after the work day ended, which was usually around 17:00 hours.

We generally took about five inmates to AA/NA meetings after the dinner count once a week. The meetings were usually held in either a hall or a church in the community. These meetings would usually last for about two hours. As escort officers, we were supposed to sit in the meetings with the inmates, thus observing the inmates under our supervision. Personally, I did not usually sit in on the meetings, as I believed that the inmates would not open up during the meeting, as that had been my experience in the past. So I would tell them that I would do spot checks on them; after all, they were in a minimum security institution and were expected to act accordingly.

This one evening, after the dinner count, the inmates that we usually took out to these types of meetings were as usual hanging outside our office waiting to go on their escort.

I noticed that there was a new guy arrival among them, who I will call Andy. Seeing that I pretty much knew everyone else, I asked one of my fellow officers on duty about him, and was informed that he has just recently been transferred in from a medium security institution. So I pulled his 1133 card, which is an identification card that we keep on every inmate in our institution. It contains a recent photo of the inmate along with their name, current sentence, past sentences and age, height, etc. We are required to take these cards with us when we take inmates out on escort, just in case something happens, such as an escape.

So with all my paperwork in hand, I grabbed the keys to the vehicle, and stepped outside. I gave them the usual lecture on behaviour and what was expected of them during the escort, and everyone clearly understood as usual, as this was not their first escort. We then all climbed into the unmarked institutional vehicle which was equipped with an institutional radio. I did my radio check as everyone got in and I noticed Andy climbing into the back seat as I could clearly see him in my rear-view mirror.

As I was driving to the meeting, I couldn't help but think, *I know this guy from somewhere. He looks very familiar.* So, looking at him in the rear-view mirror, I said, "You look very familiar to me. Have we ever met before?"

I could see him looking at me in the mirror and sensed that he too was thinking the same. He went on to say, "This I my first federal sentence."

So I asked him what he did before he came into the system, and lo and behold, he said, "I used to be a roofer when I was out on the street." As I was looking in the mirror, I couldn't help but grin. "I think you and I worked together years ago."

I could see his eyes light up and a slight grin on his face, but he did not respond. We arrived at our destination and I parked the vehicle near the entrance to the meeting. We all exited the vehicle and I followed the inmates into the building where the NA/AA meeting was being held. Once inside, each inmate grabbed a coffee and mingled with the other members in the room. So I hung around for a bit until the meeting was about to start, grabbed a coffee, and headed back to the vehicle. About 30 minutes later everyone in the meeting came out for a smoke; I visually accounted for every inmate and noticed that Andy was heading towards me.

So I got out of the vehicle and asked him if everything was alright. He said, "Oh, yeah. Everything is good. I was just sitting in the meeting when I realized who you were." And he stuck out his hand and said, "Been a long time, John. How the hell did you find yourself in corrections?"

"Well," I told him, "I had a little help from the father of an old girlfriend, and just sort of stayed with the job." We chatted for a bit, and then he headed back into the meeting. When the meeting was over, we all piled back into the institutional vehicle and headed back to the institution.

Andy was soon released some months later on day parole, and I never heard or saw him again, but realized what a small world we truly live in.

ONE ANGRY MAN

One day on afternoon shift I was working with two other officers and a supervisor, we had just finished the meal line count, and the inmates were on recreation time. We were required to do hourly rounds of the camp and park area, and usually we could sense if things were not quite right. This particular evening, we had a few in visitors in the V&C building. Later, during our walks through the units, Officer Larry and I could sense that something was up. Things just were not right on key. We noticed that there was a small gathering of inmates in another inmate's room; two were older, experienced inmates who had been around the system for many years. The other was a young inmate who had transferred in a few weeks before, and it was clear when he arrived that he had a chip on his shoulder.

They were hanging out together, and the noise factor coming from their room told Larry and I that they were into something other than coffee. We passed by the room and could not smell any brew of the sort, but we knew they were up to something.

We reported back to the office after our round, and I stepped into the coffee room to get myself a coffee. Soon thereafter, the young inmate we had seen in the room came into the office dressed in a heavy leather biker coat. Larry was standing across the counter and asked him if he was warm, as it was the middle of July and a warm evening. Again, my bells and whistles were going off.

The inmate all of a sudden became verbally abuse and was very aggressive in his physical body language. The supervisor, hearing this, came out of his office to see what was going on, and the inmate started to increase his level of aggression. Larry said, "I think you need to come into the back office and we need to talk."

The inmate, who I will call Josh, reached out as to push Larry away from him, and that was when all hell broke out.

Then Josh took a swing at the supervisor, so we all jumped on him, wrestling him to the floor. It was clear to me that he was on something, as he was not a big individual, and there were three of us trying to get him to the floor and restrained. The supervisor grabbed a set of handcuffs at some point, as Larry and I tried to take Josh to the floor. The leather jacket that he was wearing had long sleeves and was restricting us from getting the cuffs on him.

Finally, we were able to get him on the ground. One of the other officers leaned over him and put his knee on his throat; he still continued to resist. The officer told him to stop resisting. Exhausted now, Josh started to relax enough for us to get the cuffs on him.

We got him to his feet and the supervisor told Josh that he was going to be transferred to Kent Maximum Institution. We had our security van parked alongside of the duty office and he was placed in the back and secured.

We were catching our breaths, standing outside the side door of our office, when all of a sudden, we heard a large bang coming from the van. Josh was kicking the side door from the inside of the van. Then there was a large bang as the side window exploded as he kicked out the window. Small pieces of glass flew everywhere in our direction.

He then started to yell profanities at us. "You're all fucking assholes. Just wait 'til I get out of these cuffs. You're all dead." I looked over at my supervisor and he went inside the office and returned with a can of pepper spray. He told Josh, "If you don't behave yourself, I'll use this on you." Josh's response was a little quieter, and I assumed he had had it used on him before.

The supervisor gave the pepper spray to Larry and said, "Stay here and keep an eye on him, while I go in and do the transfer papers for Kent."

Moments later, I hopped into the driver's seat, and Larry and I were heading down our access road to Kent Institution. We were just about to drive across the bridge over the Harrison River, when Josh was lying on the bench seat and started kicking the side door with both his feet. I looked over my right shoulder and could see that every time he kicked it, it almost came open. Seeing that he was clearly under the influence of something, I was guessing that he would probably try and jump out of the van as we were going over the bridge, which would not end well for him.

Larry must have read my mind as he had the pepper spray in his hand and was telling the inmate that if he didn't stop, he would give him a shot. And as the inmate lined himself up to kick the door again, Larry gave him a two burst of pepper spray. The only problem with that was Josh had already kicked out the side window. When Larry gave him a shot, it backfired as the wind blow it in our direction.

We both immediately opened both of our windows and struck our heads out to relieve the burning pain in our eyes.

Meanwhile, the inmate had stopped kicking the door only to begin bashing his head against the steel cage that separated us. He then ripped a piece of the moulding off the ceiling of the van and tried to poke me with it through the side of the cage.

Larry grabbed it and pulled it into the front of the van. Then Larry gave him another shot of pepper spray, and Josh started to bang his head against the security screen again and again. The next time his face was pressed up against the screen that separated us, Larry gave him a clear shot in his face. Inmate Josh sat back on the bench seat and that seemed to calm him down a little.

The night before, inmate Josh had had a visit from his girlfriend, and when she left early I sensed that they'd had a fight, so I asked, "How is your girlfriend? And how was your visit with her last night?"

Well, within minutes of me asking him, he sat back on the bench seat, and started to talk about his girlfriend and the fight that they'd had the night before. Apparently, she was mad at him for being picked up for breaking his parole. We talked about this and that, and I kept talking to him until we pulled up to Kent Institution. I asked him if he was going to okay and he said that he was fine.

We passed through the double gates, and headed towards the Admission and Discharge building. As we pulled up, the back door opened and the afternoon keeper, with whom I had worked back in BC Pen, greeted us at the door. As he stepped out, he was followed by at least six very large correctional officers, and one of them had a video camera to record anything that happened.

It was obvious to me that our supervisor had called Kent and told them what to expect when we arrived. The officers made a circle round the side door of the van. I stepped to one side, unlocked it, and pulled the door open. Inmate Josh stepped out of the van as calm as could be, but it was clear that he had numerous cuts and abrasions around his face and on his forehead from banging his head on the metal cage. The six officers escorted him into A&D, keeping him well within reach in case he acted up again.

It was decided once we were inside that inmate Josh would be taken to health care to be seen by the nurse before he was placed in segregation. At that point Larry and I turned to return to our van, when the keeper called me aside, and said, "Damn, Cookie. Did you have to beat him to subdue him."

I just laughed and said, "He did all of that to himself when he was in the van on the way here. All we did was just talk him down prior to our arrival."

Soon thereafter, Larry and I returned to our institution; with the smell of pepper spray lingering on our clothing and throughout the security van. What a night that was.

GROUP PASSES

Before Elbow Lake became a Native healing village, we used to take out group passes in the community on the evening shift. There were usually limited to five inmates at a time, and we would post what passes and where they were for on the bulletin board by the inmate kitchen.

Each inmate, of course, would have to be approved for any type of temporary absence prior to applying for any group pass. There were two types of conditional release: escorted temporary absence (ETA) or unescorted temporary absence (UTA). This type of release was usually authorized for various reasons, such as work in the community, service projects, or family contact, and personal development and medical.

Most inmates may apply for ETAs at anytime during their sentence, and most ETAs were at the discretion of the CSC, with the exception of those who are serving a life sentence and first have to be approved by the National Parole Board.

Personally, for me, these evening ETAs were the most enjoyable, as it gave me a break from working in the institution. And every officer, of course, enjoyed different types of events, ranging from a hockey games to shopping, movies, etc.

My personal three favourites were shopping passes, movie passes and roller skating, I personally never had a bad ETA, but remember one incident, though, where things could have gone badly.

ROLLER SKATING

At the time I was taking five inmates out into the community to the roller skating rink, I was living with a woman who had two young children, a boy and a girl. My girlfriend knew that I would be at the roller rink that evening with five inmates. She took it upon herself to take her children to the rink, at the same time that she knew I would be there.

We arrived at the rink, and we all went in and got our skates and found a table close to the rink. We were just lacing up when she and the kids arrived. I was little surprised, but seeing that I knew the five inmates, wasn't really concerned security-wise, and we were only going to be there for a few hours, I didn't see any harm in it.

The five inmates that were with me had been in the correctional system ranging from five years to life; four of them I had known back in my time in Kent Institution. The other, Butch, was serving five years for aggravated assault and was affiliated with the Hells Angels. He was a broad man in his mid-30s and stood about six feet four inches. I had worked closely with him during the summer when he was on my fire fighting crew. He was in great physical shape, generally easy going, and always cooperative.

The girlfriend and the kids came over to the table and Butch stood up and stuck out his hand and said, "Hi, I'm Butch. It's nice to meet you."

Then my girlfriend reached out and shook his hand, and to my surprise they all stepped up and introduced themselves. Then Butch looked at me and said, "See you on the rink," and all five of them headed out on the rink.

I helped the youngest get her skates on. She was a cute little thing, always smiling, and very friendly with everyone. She was very intelligent and mature for her young age. Her three-year-older brother was independent, and was quite the artist for his age. He loved to sketch and was exceptionally talented at artwork and enjoyed dawning gothic cartoons.

Once the two of them had their skates on, they headed out to the rink. The youngest was a slower skater than her brother and a little uneasy on her skates. She was skating all by herself along the edge of the rink.

I wasn't too concerned until I noticed a young man go by our table, dodging people as he skated around the rink. As he was coming up to where the youngest was skating next to the wall, he came awfully close to her then was cut off by another skater. He came so close to her that he startled her and she fell.

The next thing I knew, Butch was skating over to her and was helping her up to her feet. I headed over right away, followed closely by her mother. When we arrived, her mother asked if she was okay or hurt, and she said, "No, I just looked up and there he was, really close to me, and I just lost my balance."

The next thing I knew, Butch turned and was skating after the young man, who now was now halfway around the area on the other side. I immediately skated directly across the area and up next to Butch, and said, "She's okay. Thanks for helping her out, but right now you need to go have a smoke." He looked at me and knew what I was saying, and then looked over and stared at the young man with a very firm look, then headed off the rink.

I looked over and saw the girlfriend skating hand in hand with her daughter as they headed back to the table. We all sat around for about 20 minutes and then the youngest wanted to skate some more and headed out on her own, followed shortly by Butch. I paid no never mind, as the young man who was racing around, had left.

The next time I looked up, I saw the youngest being pulled around the area, hanging on to the back of Butch's T-shirt. The girlfriend thought that was pretty cute, as it was apparent that he was in his own way protecting her from other aggressive skaters.

The rest of the escort went without any more incidents and we returned to the institution as scheduled.

Some three months later, Butch was released on day parole. A few months after that, I was working my last day on afternoon shift. I got relieved early, and so I decided to stop in at the local bar on my way home for a beer. It was Tuesday, and when I pulled into the parking lot, it was pretty empty. I only saw a few vehicles and a motorcycle in the parking lot. As I exited my vehicle, I couldn't help but notice that the bike was a relatively new Harley, black with an outstanding blue and white mural on the tank of a half-naked woman.

I headed up the stairs and into the pub. Looking around as I walked through the doors, I noticed three very young attractive women sitting around a table next to a fireplace. I proceeded up the bar, and started chatting with the bartender that I knew. All of a sudden, someone stepped up behind me, wrapped his arms around me, started squeezing me tightly, and then proceeded to bounce me up and down like a rag doll, "Cookie, it's great to see you."

I immediately knew it was Butch, and said, "For fuck's sake, put me down before you break my ribs." He immediately released me and spun me around and gave me a hug. I could smell the alcohol on his breath.

"Good to see you too, Butch. How are things with you?" It was obvious that he'd had a few to drink, and was excited to see me.

He then pointed over to the three women sitting around a table next to the fireplace, and said, "All is good. Come join us for a beer, and if you would like one of these young ladies, just help yourself."

I just laughed and said, "Remember, I have a girlfriend who I'm living with, but I'll join you for a quick one, as she's waiting for me at home." I sat at the table and listened to his stories of being back out on the streets for about 40 minutes before excusing myself.

As I stood up to leave, he reached out, gave me a shoulder hug, and said, "Take care, Cookie." I said the same and left.

Some three years later, when I was regional president of our newly founded union, I was touring Mission Institution one sunny day when I ran into Butch one last time. He was not the man I remembered from some three to four years before; he looked a little older, drawn in the face, and had put on a few pounds. We had a chance to chat and catch up, and that's when he told me that he was in serving a life sentence.

Since my retirement, I have run into a few ex-offenders that I knew on the street, and I have always been greeted with the utmost respect.

CHAPTER 10

UCCO-SACC-CSN

credit: UCCO-SACC-CSN

The "Union of Canadian Correctional Officers," was founded in Montreal, Quebec, on January 19, 1999, it is a democratic non-profitable antonymous employee organization affiliated with the Confédération des syndicats nationaux (CSN).

When I first started in the Penitentiary Service of Canada in 1977, we were affiliated with Public Service Alliance of Canada (PSAC).

THE BEGINNING OF UCCO-SACC-CSN

There were three major components that contributed to the success of our newly founded union, the first one being the CSN, which is based in Montreal and was founded in 1921. The CSN has improved the working conditions and lives of thousands of Quebec workers. They also have very experienced personnel, ranging from advisors, lawyers, actuaries, economists, health and safety, communication, mobilization, and every regional officer across Canada had an experienced advisor and secretary. This, along with their financial help, made our union become one of the strongest unions today.

The second component was the simple fact that our union was represented by experienced correctional officers who had numerous years of experience working in various institutions across Canada.

The third component was that we were at the time negotiating our contact at the federal level with the senior deputy commissioner, Don Head, who was also at one time a correctional officer, and had been appointed by the then-commissioner to negotiate the first global agreement ever at the federal level.

It all began in the late 90s. A large majority of correctional officers had become disillusioned with our current union, the PSAC. Many of us were under the impression that we could not separate from the PSAC; there were 160,000 members in PSAC, and only 2% of those were correctional officers.

So a handful of correctional officers took it upon themselves to approach the CSN, wanting to see if it was possible to break away from PSAC and create our own union, one that would be represented by correctional officers.

In early 1999, dedicated members were recruited in all 54 institutions across the country to organize a union raid campaign; it would take a majority vote of correctional officers to overturn the alliance, and unfortunately the first attempt was unsuccessful because the government extended the contract for one more year to block the raid. In 2000, the CSN, however, organized a second raid; this time they got more aggressive and UCCO-SACC-CSN organized information lines in front of every one of the 54 institutions across Canada. On May 25, 2000, UCCO-SACC-CSN filed a motion to be certified, and finally in March 2001, after a vote of 70% of correctional officers across Canada, UCCO-SACC-CSN was born.

LOCAL PRESIDENT

In 2003, I was elected as the local president of Kwìkwèxwelhp Healing Lodge. Andy, from William Head Institution, was the regional president at the time. I was attending my first national convention in 2004 in Ontario as the local president of my institution. Andy had decided not to run again, and out of the nine local presidents attending, no one wanted to volunteer to step up to fill the position.

It was getting down to election time, and BC was the only region that had no candidate running. We were all sitting around a table at the convention the morning before elections closed, and someone said, "Cookie why don't you run for regional president, seeing that you've been in the service for a good many years." I really had no idea what I was in for, but I stepped up to the plate.

Newly elected National Executive 2004. credit: UCCO-SACC-CSN
Starting from left to right, myself, Kevin Grabowski, Jason Godin, Sylvain Martel, Doug Hayhurst, Paul Harrigan, Pierre Dumont.

Most of the national executive had been together since the conception of our union, with the exception of Pierre Dumont and myself.

My first experience with the national executive was shortly after the national general assembly. I had to be in Ottawa as we were scheduled to meet with the Commissioner of Corrections Canada. At the last moment, we were informed that he could not attend, and that we would be meeting with the Deputy

Commissioner of Corrections, Don Head. Don had started his CSC career as a correctional officer at Williams Head Institution in Victoria, BC, on February 1, 1978. He took on a series of operational and managerial positions which took him to four institutions, and eventually he ended up at national headquarters in Ottawa.

We had met on occasion back in the early 80s, while he was working at Kent Institution. I knew very little about him at the time, but what I did learn over the years was he was an honourable man and he was proud of where he came from, that being the correctional ranks.

When he eventually became Commission of Corrections Canada on June 27, 2008, it was a day that the entire national executive celebrated. Being a ranking officer, Don understood the job we did, and knew that our union was represented by ranking officers who had served years of experience at various institutional security levels.

At the time of the meeting, I was sitting across the table from Don; we shook hands as he welcomed me to my new position. We had a few good chuckles as we exchanged a few stories of our time in corrections.

A few of my brother union officers looked a little concerned about how friendly I was with him, causing the national president to remark, "Seems to me that you are pretty friendly with Don."

I said, "Well we did meet a few times over the years. Seeing that he was originally one of us at one point, I have the upmost respect for him working his way up from our ranks to where he is today."

It was tough go the first year with the executive. They were trying to figure out who I was and where I stood. But they learned, in time, that my heart and commitment were in the right place. I believed, since I had worked in the service for some 27 years, and had worked at various institutional levels that included a newly formed healing village, that would garner me some level of respect. But, as they say, respect is earned, and this was so true with the national executive.

It brought me back to my first days when I started out as a rookie guard in at BC Penitentiary. Most of the guards, as we used to call ourselves back in the day, were experienced, and they were a very tight group who had their own way of doing things. New ideas don't come easy to most correctional officers, and trust only comes with time and experience. In the first year of being at the national table, I was treated pretty much like a rookie.

2004 - HARD TIME

Since I first started in the penitentiary service, guards were not allowed to talk about their job or incidents that happened behind the walls. Not complying meant facing serious discipline charges or dismissal. With the conception of our new union, this was all going to change for the better; the Canadian public was now going to know who we are and what we represented.

In 2004, our union started a national visibility campaign, which came to be known across Canada as Hard Time. This project was designed to open the doors on what really happens behind those four walls, and what is it that correctional officers do every day, as well as what kind of dangers they could face each day on the job. The campaign was aimed at attracting the attention of the general public as well as the law enforcement community to the difficult and dangerous nature of the job correctional officers do every day. Officers perform "extreme social work" that is indispensable for society, but they do so without the tools and considerations necessary to the tasks that they face every day.

UCCO-SACC-CSN GOES PUBLIC

2004 Hard Time press release, credit: UCCO-SACC-CSN

HARD TIME PRESS RELEASE

There were several reasons why we went public, the first one being that we wanted to get our image out there and let the citizens of Canada know who we are, and that we are professionals much like police officers and fire fighters and first responders. The second reason was to let the Canadian public know that we had been in negotiations for a collective agreement with the Federal Government of Canada for over three years. The union had over 80 negotiation sessions at that time with the government, yet had have only settled half of what we had in our bargaining contact.

We wanted such things as better working conditions and better training. We wanted to be involved in what type of training correctional officers received. Things had changed over the years, and with more and more gangs emerging in our jails and the increase in gang-related incidents, we needed to have a system in place where these individuals could be identified—who they are, how they work within and outside of our jails—in order to make our jails safer for everyone, including the inmates. We also wanted leave with pay for pregnant female correctional officers. Schedules were also an issue; since I first started in the service in 1977, there was only one schedule. We were working seven days on, three days off, then seven days on and four days off; thus, we wanted better work schedules, to improve our quality of life. Regarding health and safety, we wanted the tools to make sure we were safe while working. We wanted stab-proof vests. If we were scratched or body fluids were thrown on us, we wanted to know if that inmate had AIDS/HIV or any other communicable diseases so we could get the proper medical attention and to be able to better protect ourselves.

AN OPERATION IN FIVE STEPS

The campaign was expressed in five slogans and five themes that explained the situation and needs of correctional officers. These five themes constituted an exercise that departed from common stereotypes on a voyage of discovery of the dangerous place where officers work. The voyage explored the impacts on their private lives before arriving at the necessary recognition of the essential role they perform in our society and the indispensable tools they needed.

SPEAKING OUT

Speaking in a single voice from one end of the country to the other, correctional officers expressed the need to tell the public who they are, how they live, and what they need in order to accomplish their mission. In the first magazine, 16 correctional officers from the five regions of Canada lifted the veil on their unique and sometimes misunderstood world. Their testimonials were an appeal to the public's sense of justice and social responsibility.

2005 - WE ARE STILL DOING HARD TIME

In the summer of 2005, the federal government released statistics to the media claiming that there had been only one major assault against a Correctional Service staff (including but not limited to correctional officers) in the previous four years. While statistics can be endlessly manipulated, this claim was breathtaking.

Even by CSC's own definitions, the number was ridiculous. CSC records a major assault against staff as one that causes an injury of a serious nature that results in hospitalization or treatment, which prohibits the victim's return to normal routine for any period of time. This includes cuts requiring sutures (depending on the severity), unconsciousness, broken bones, etc. By that measure, there had been at least 83 major assaults in the previous year alone. But even the definition is arbitrary. It does not capture, for instance, assaults with bodily fluids, feces, urine, saliva, semen, or blood, which can be deadly in an environment with sky-high infections rates of HIV and Hepatitis A, B, C, and D. Nor did they capture the psychological injuries caused by incidents such as a hostage-taking, even if no physical damage was caused. For correctional officers on the receiving end of those forms of assault, however, these are anything but minor. Worst of all, CSC did not even record the on-duty killing of Yellowknife parole officer Louise Pargeter in the fall of the previous year.

It was pretty clear from this that the federal government really wanted to keep us hidden from the public. We felt that they had no respect for what correctional officers do and go though on a daily basis, and they continued to keep the general public blind as to what was happening in jails across Canada.

Our union was relentless. We kept up the pressure through information lines and media releases, along with chasing down our members of parliament and explaining to them who we were, and how the government was not living up to sitting down at the bargaining table in good faith.

2005 GLOBAL AGREEMENT

In 2005, UCCO-SACC-CSN worked on the first two-tiered negotiations between the Treasury Board and CSC; it was a historic millstone agreement that resolved a lot of labour relations and operational issues that we were having at the time. We met with the deputy commissioner, Don Head, at the Ontario UCCO-SACC-CSN regional office; we arranged to meet with the deputy commissioner over the weekends. Over long hours, many discussions took place, and then finally we reached an agreement. The provisions contained in the global agreement were not subject to grievances, but rather to a distinct dispute resolution process. The global agreement would come into effect with the signing of the new collective agreement and would continue to be in effect until the next signing of the next new agreement.

It was the first of its kind, and an historic millstone for our union.

I understand how much work each and every one of us at the national table put into our union—long hours, and lots of committees. Many members did not really have the time away from their daily responsibilities to take holidays, as we were in the middle of contract negotiations.

Two years later, and after a lot of hard work, we signed off on our first collective agreement for UCCO-SACC-CSN.

I stepped down as the regional president of BC in 2007, and took the position of Regional Vice President for the next three years. I was coming up to my 31 years in the CSC, and as much as I enjoyed working for the union and representing my region, I wanted to spend my remaining years back on the front lines until I retired. I was a line officer; it was just in my blood. I returned to my previous institution, Kwìkwèxwelhp Healing Lodge. I was also in the mind set of thinking that it was time for the new and up-and-coming officers to take the reins and step up and represent their fellow officers.

2006 The National Executive, credit: UCCO-SACC-CSN

Myself, 2006. Signing the first collective agreement of UCCO-SACC-CSN, credit UCCO-SACC-CSN

CHAPTER 11

LATE NIGHT CALL

Late one chilly evening in December 2008, I was at home, snuggled comfortably in my bed, when the phone rang, I looked over at the clock on my side table and noted the time, 22:30. Picking up the phone, I said, "Hello."

The voice on the other end, said, "Hi, Cookie. This is John here at Kent. We have a situation and we need your help.

Sitting up now, totally wide awake, I said, "Okay, what's going on? Talk to me?

John went on to say, "We have an officer who is AWOL. His wife came home about an hour ago, and found a suicide note on the kitchen table. There was also a cardboard box and a receipt for a 12 gauge shotgun.

"He was supposed to report for graveyard, but hasn't reported in. The keeper has minimum-staffed the institution and we have some staff driving around Agassiz looking for him and his vehicle. The RCMP has been notified, but no one knows where he could possibly be. We were thinking if maybe you could a drive around your area and see if maybe you can spot his minivan."

"Sure, let me get a pen and a piece of paper." I took down the information, got dressed, and headed out the door. I drove around my area where people usually hung out, but turned nothing up. I then decided to take drive up the east side of the lake that I lived on, and then came to a Y. To this day I don't know why I turned down the other road, but I did. It was mid-December, cold and icy, especially up at higher elevations, I continued down the road, noticing that the snow was getting a little higher. When I came around a corner, I spotted a dark-coloured minivan parked sideways on the road.

I pulled up a few car lengths away and, leaving my truck running, grabbed a flashlight and headed towards the van. It was covered in frost and the side windows were covered in ice. I came around back of the van and shined my flashlight on the licence plate. *Yep, this was the van.* I walked along the driver's side, and at the angle it was parked, I could see a large hole in the front window. At that point, I was thinking, *Oh, shit. When I open this door, I'm half expecting to find a dead body.* I took a deep breath and reached for the door handle.

Just as my fingertips touched the chrome handle, the door popped open. A little surprised, I took a step back. There inside was a tall, slim man, shaking from the cold. He had no shoes on, and a light summer jacket. Between his legs was a shotgun with the barrel facing up in the direction of the hole in the front window.

"Hi, you know there are a lot of people worried about you."

He just looked at me blindly.

"Do you know who I am?"

He looked up at me and said, "Yes, you're John Williams. You're the regional vice president of our union."

"Yes, and I need you to do me a big favour right now. I want you to gently hand me that shotgun."

He looked at the gun and then, pointing the barrel away from me, he handed it to me through the door, stock first.

I took the shotgun and stepped back, pointing it in the opposite direction and cocked the action. There were no live shells in the chamber or barrel. I immediately took a big sigh of relief. I looked at him and said, "Do you have any more shells?"

He looked down, and said, "Yes." With his left hand reached up and handed me a single red 12-gauge shotgun shell.

"Is this it?"

"It's the last one," he responded.

"Well, buddy, you look pretty cold, so how about we get you out of here and to some place warm? What do you think?"

He didn't argue with me. He reached in behind his seat, grabbed his already wet shoes, stood up, closed the van door, and followed me back to my truck. I opened the door for him, and he got in passenger seat. I went around to the driver's side, opened up my back door, and placed the shotgun on the floor, the single shell still in shoved into my pocket, and hopped in. I was not sure what to say to him at this point, but I did let him know that there would be a lot of people happy to know that he was okay. I was out of cell service at the time, and would have to wait until we got back to my house to make a call.

As I turned the truck around, I turned up the heat in the truck. "So, how are you feeling?"

"I'm a little cold. I ran out of gas, and tried to walk back down the road, but it was too cold and windy, so I just came back to the van."

"Well, we'll go to my place," I said, "and I'll put on some coffee and get you warmed up."

All my years in the service and the courses we took for suicide prevention never prepared me for this. I was fine other than I really didn't want to say the wrong thing, not knowing how stable he was. So I just kept the conversation light on the way home. We talked about how long he had worked at Kent Institution, his hobbies, and by that time we arrived at my residence. I pulled into the driveway and said, "Well, let's get you out of this cold."

He followed me to the front door, and I pointed over at the couch and said, "Have a seat, and I'll put some coffee on. I also have to make a few calls. Are you okay with that?"

"Yes, of course," he responded. "I understand."

I called the institution and notified the keeper that I had found him, and to let his wife know that he was safe and sound at my house with me, and to also let his crew know.

Approximately 30 minutes later, four of his friends and crew members arrived at my residence with beer in hand. They came in pleased see that their bother in arms was okay. We chatted for a bit, and then about 20 minutes later, I received a phone call from the RCMP, asking me if I was in possession of the shotgun. I stated that I did have it in my possession.

The officer stated that they were on their way and would be arriving at my residence shortly. Approximately 20 minutes later, the RCMP officer again called me from his cell phone and asked if I could meet him in my driveway. I said sure, and after hanging up the phone, I told his crew that I had to go out and hand over the shotgun to the RCMP.

As I was walking out to meet with the officer, now parked in my driveway, I noticed an ambulance next to his police car. The officer introduced himself and as I handed over the shotgun to him, he stated that he was the one I had been communicating with earlier. "Was the gun loaded?"

I said, "No, the gun was empty when he gave it to me."

The officer took my statement, then said, "Due to the fact that this incident was an attempted suicide, the officer will have to be checked out by the paramedics, and then he'll be taken to Chilliwack General Hospital for psychological assessment."

"I understand. Would you give me a few minutes to explain this to him?"

The officer understood. "We'd just like to make sure he's safe."

Back into the house, I got the guys together and explained what was going to happen. The officer was a little upset; he just wanted to go home. After some explaining, he understood. We exited the house, followed by all his fellow brother officers, to the waiting RCMP officer, who explained to him again what was going to happen. The officer was then placed in the ambulance and taken to Chilliwack General Hospital.

After everyone had gone, I sat on my front porch with a glass of red wine, looking out over the lake. I was thankful that I found him when I did. If I had been five minutes later, the situation might have been far worse.

I kept that shotgun shell for years; I was deeply saddened to learn that some five years later, the same officer eventually took his own life, not far from where I was living at the time.

I never found out the circumstances surrounding his death, but I do know that many of my fellow officers suffer from post-traumatic stress disorder.

Someone once said, "As hard as it is not to feel pain, sometimes it's even more difficult not to."

CHAPTER 12

POST-TRAUMATIC STRESS DISORDER

The medical textbook description of post-traumatic stress disorder (PTSD) is that it's a mental health condition that's triggered by a terrifying event (TE), either experiencing it or witnessing it. Symptoms may include flashbacks, nightmares, and severe anxiety, as well and uncontrollable thoughts about the event that one had experienced. In reality, most correctional officer who begin their career will witness things that they have never seen before, and the more time they spend inside those four walls, the more they will eventually see.

The inmates we work with every day come from all walks of life. A large majority are basically violent people, who also suffer from various levels of violence and mental health and drug addiction issues.

There was a study done in the Quebec region back in 2002 and 2004. It showed that in 2004, correctional officers in Quebec were more likely to present signs of psychological distress linked with work when they were exposed to high psychological demands, low decision latitude, job strain, and poor social support from superiors and colleagues. Psychological distress was also shown to be greater when reward at work was scarce and when there was an imbalance between effort and reward at work. Finally, in 2004, psychological distress among correctional officers was also associated with intimidation and psychological harassment at the workplace.

Personally, I honestly didn't know when I retired if I personally suffered from PTSD after being subjected to years of violence and extreme events.

Working as a correctional officer to me was good, honourable work. I enjoyed working as a team member and I enjoyed the challenges of my job. But when you're subject to seeing what every correctional officer sees over the years, it can and will affect you—there's no two ways about it—and it does affect you mentally.

I attended a union convention once, where a psychologist gave a lecture on PTSD and the mental status of correctional officers. She stated to an assembly of some 150 correctional officers that at least half of those in attendance have suffered some form of PTSD during their course of employment.

Well, once she said that, you could have heard a pin drop in that assembly.

She went on to say that correctional officers had the highest PTSD stats across Canada.

PTSD was first recognized after the return of those who served in the Vietnam War in the 1970s; PTSD was not officially recognized until 1980, some ten years later.

Due to the nature of our job, many correctional officers may not realize that they suffer from PTSD. For those correctional officers who are suffering with it today, know that you are not alone. There are many of your brothers and sisters out there who are dealing with it every day. But there are resources available. All you have to do is just reach out and ask for help.

Times have changed since I started as a correctional officer back in 1977. PTSD was not something that was ever openly recognized among my fellow officers. We just worked through it as best we could. We were our own support group, and therefore talked about it among ourselves, usually over beers after shift at one of the local pubs.

All this actually did was create more problems in other areas, such as alcoholism and drug abuse. These were not healthy ways of dealing with PTSD, but I wrote it off to just being part of the job. Unfortunately, these types of coping skills were more like putting a bandage on a severe wound; it was only a temporary fix.

PTSD is not just limited to those who are soldiers, police officers, or first responders; it affects many other people from all walks of life in general.

Again, speaking for myself, I found over the years that some people could handle a lot of stress on the job, and some, not so much. This by no means should be taken as a negative comment; it just means that some people are a little more resilient than others.

Back when I was working in the BC Penitentiary, I remember that a lot of the officers I worked with were ex military or various law enforcement agencies. These officers had already seen their fair share of traumatic incidents in their time. Thus, they had developed thicker skin, so to speak, and had already had their own personal coping mechanisms in place that worked for them.

The symptoms of PTSD vary from one person to another, and here I can only speak for myself as to my understanding of what I went through after I retired.

After I retired and was working on this book, I suddenly came to realize, while writing this article, that soon after I retired I had developed avoidance behaviour issues. What does this mean? It means that I subconsciously stayed clear of anything or anyone that reminded me of what I went through during my 36 years in corrections.

Realizing this, it started to make me think. So one day, I was talking to a long-time close friend and ex-partner who I worked with for many years. I went on to tell him that I had come to the realization, while working on the PTSD part of my book, that I might have developed some issues that were not apparent at the time when I retired.

During our conversation, I asked him, "Who do you socialize with from work?"

Before he could answer I went on to say, "We worked for years inside, and during that time, we got to know a lot of officers, who we socialized with on and off the job, and who we came to consider friends as well, which created a bond between us. But since you have retired who do you socialize with now?"

Well, he looked at me and said, "Just you."

We both sat there for a minute thinking, and we both came to the same conclusion as I stated earlier: we probably both suffered from some form of post-traumatic stress.

Working in a correction environment, you will, over time, build strong working relationships with people you work closely with on a daily basis. You have to, after all, rely on one another and work together as partners and as a team. You work in an environment that is negative, not to mention you are working with criminals from all walks of life and backgrounds, and the chances of being subjected to violence are a day-to-day possibility.

Now, depending on one's severity of PTSD symptoms, the textbook says that it can also lead to the development of mental disorders to cope with the constant flight or fight state of mind. Personally, at the end of my career, I found myself getting somewhat irritable, and at times had sudden feelings of anger for no apparent reason.

I also came to realize that if something was going on in my life that I had very little control over, or something affected me emotionally, I would think about it over and over.

I would go to sleep, then find myself waking up the following day . . . and the first thing that I would think about as I opened my eyes was the thought that I had been struggling with.

I would play it back through my mind over and over again, which resulted in me getting irritable and edgy. I realized that this was not healthy for me. So, going back to what I said about coping skills, I fell back into doing what I had always done when I needed to take that edge off—I started to work out again, to the point where I was physically and mentally exhausted.

I would go for long walks up a mountain path for about an hour and a half every morning; it helped me clear my head, and allowed me to deal with what I was feeling in a more positive way.

★   ★   ★

When I was around 16 years old and living with my father and stepmother, I also suffered from sudden outbursts and anger issues, which I now realize were due to changes in my life: my father remarrying and moving out of my grandparents' home; moving into a new home and living with my step-mother; not to mention the fact that my sister had recently moved out of our family home and was now living with my mother and her husband in North Vancouver.

The next weekend I went to visit my mother in North Vancouver, the following morning my mom woke me up to tell me that she was going to take me to doctor to have an aptitude test done.

Well, I was 16 at the time, and really didn't understand why I needed this, let alone what it was truly about, but I cheerfully got up and got ready. Once we arrived at the doctor's office, I failed to notice the writing on his glass window, which stated "Dr. Smith, Psychiatrist."

Once inside, he introduced himself to me, and asked me to take a seat in a chair across from his. He started to ask me questions about issues that I was having with school, and if I ever felt anger towards others, and how did I fell about being separated from my sister and living with my father and my stepmother.

Well, I finally came to realize that there was no test; apparently, as I found out in my later years, that this was co-arranged between my mother and father, to have me assessed for my teenage anger issues.

Everyone who suffers from a traumatic incident may not see it themselves, but others close to you will see changes in your behaviour that are not normal. My behaviour issues at the time were due to dealing with the separation and divorce of my mother and father, and then having to deal with someone else who came into my father's life, who tried to fill that role of my mother.

HOW LONG WILL PTSD LAST?

Well, the textbook version says, it all depends on the original response that an individual has to the trauma-related event and what type of treatment they receive. Personally, when I was younger, I came to realize that I need to learn how to open up and communicate and express my feelings and emotions in a positive manner.

At 19 years of age, I had just joined the Canadian Navy and was on leave for a few days and would be spending it with my mother. She very much knew that I still was struggling with anger issues; my behaviour was to say a little erratic at times.

We were sitting at the table having dinner one evening, and she looked up at me and said, "Johnny, I'm worried about you. I know you're still having anger issues. I'd like you to meet someone who could possibly help you deal with your anger."

I thought, *Oh, yeah. Here we go again.*

But she actually surprised the hell out of me, and sent me to someone who introduced me to transcendental meditation (TM). TM is a technique, which originated in India, for avoiding distracting thoughts and promoting a state of relaxed awareness. You are given a mantra, which is a word or sound that is used to focus your concentration. It is something that you can never share with anyone else; it is used solely for you.

It took me a while to get the hang of it, but eventually the more I meditated the deeper, more relaxed state of mind I achieved. I found myself emerged in a state of relaxation that is hard to explain in writing. But during that deep level of meditation, I found that negative thoughts just floated up out my mind, and it truly did help me to deal with the anger that I was feeling.

Normally, it would take 20 to 30 minutes to meditate, and it had to be in an area where there were no distractions, and in a place that was completely quite.

I got away from meditating over the years when I was in corrections, but I have recently started again after all these years. I find that it calms my mind and thoughts and helps me to focus more clearly. And although I do not think that I have recurring issues, I find that it allows me to feel at peace with myself and those around me.

During my time in the service, I came to realize that many of my fellow officers suffered from PTSD, and extreme stress. It took the CSC years to finally recognize it, but with the help of our union, UCCO-SACC-CSN, it is now recognized today.

Educating oneself on methods and training that are available to officers is my best advice to cope with extreme stress.

CHAPTER 13

WHEN GOD MADE CORRECTION OFFICERS

When the Lord was creating CORRECTION OFFICERS, he was into his sixth day of 16 hour overtime when an angel appeared and said, "You're doing a lot of fiddling around on this one." And the Lord said, "Have you read the specs on this order?"

A CORRECTION OFFICER must always bear in mind that rehabilitation is based on self-respect. In the event of rebellious actions or disparaging remarks towards them by inmates they must always maintain a quite firm demeanor.

A CORRECTIONAL OFFICER has to be able to tolerate the ignorance of some, without losing hope.

A CORRECTIONAL OFFICER must also be prepared to cover a life-threatening situation, canvass the institution for witnesses, write a perfect report, and testify the next day.

A CORRECTIONAL OFFICER has to be in top physical condition at all times, running on black coffee and half-eaten meals when it is necessary.

A CORRECTIONAL OFFICER has to have six pairs of hands.

The angel shook her head slowly and said, "Six pairs of hands... no way!" "It's not the hands that are causing me problems," said the Lord, "it's the three pairs of eyes an Officer has to have." "Is that on the standard model?" asked the angel.

The Lord nodded and said, "One pair that sees through a bulge in a pocket before the Officer asks, 'May I see what's in there, sir?' (When the Officer already knows and wishes he'd taken that accounting job.)" The second pair, here in the side of his head for his fellow Officers safety and the third pair of eyes here in front that can look reassuringly at a bleeding victim and say, "You'll be all right, when the Officer knows it isn't so."

"Lord," said the angel, touching his sleeve, "rest and work on this tomorrow," "I can't," said the Lord, "I already have a model that can talk a 250 pound inmate out of a rebellious intention without incident and feed a family of five on a civil service paycheck." The angel circled the model of the CORRECTIONAL OFFICER very slowly, "Can it think?" the angel asked.

The Lord said "Can it think!" A CORRECTIONAL OFFICER can recite departmental rules in its sleep; detain, investigate, search, and arrest a gang member on a tier in less time than it takes five Federal Judges to debate the legality of a cell search… and still it keeps its sense of humor. "This CORRECTIONAL OFFICER also has phenomenal personal control."

A CORRECTIONAL OFFICER can deal with crime scenes painted in hell, professionally watch over a child abuser not allowing emotions to stand in the way of helping a inmate better himself, comfort a fellow Officers family with a loss, and then read in the daily paper how the department and its Officers are not sensitive to the rights of inmates.

Finally, the angel bent over and ran her finger across the cheek of the CORRECTION OFFICER. "There's a leak," the angel pronounced. "I told you that you were trying to put too much into this model!" the angel exclaimed.

"That's not a leak," said the Lord, "it's a tear"

"What's the tear from?" asked the angel.

"It's for bottled-up emotions, for fallen comrades.

"You're a genius," said the angel.

The Lord looked somber and said, "I didn't put that tear there."

- Unknown Author

Correctional Staff Memorial

During my 36 years in the service, we unfortunately lost a good many correctional officers, before or shortly after they retired. It has been my personal experience that about 40% or higher of correctional officers who retire don't make it to their 70s.

So this is my dedication page to those who I had the honour of knowing and who I also had the honour of having worked beside during my 36 years as a correctional officer.

A Correctional Officer's Prayer

Lord, when it's time to go inside, that place of steel and stone.
I pray that you will keep me safe, so I won't walk alone.
Help me to do my duty, please watch me on my rounds.
Amongst those perilous places, and slamming steel door sounds.
God, keep my fellow officers well and free from harm.
Let them know I'll be there too, whenever there's alarm.
Above all when I walk my beat, no matter where I roam.
Let me go back whence I came, to family and home.

~ unknown author

In memory of

Bob Adams
Wendel Amon
Ken Anderson
Roger Asslin
Cathy Antell
Bob Blakeway
Tom Beason
Joe Beauchane
Gary Blount
Steve Bonnett
Mary Boycott
Harvey Boycott
Matt Brown
Joe Butcher
Jack Byers
Mike Clayton
Morgan Collette
Ted Connor
Jim Cowie
Tom Croizer
Cliff DeGrasse
Gene Desibecker
John Dowsett
Ambe Duperon
Rena Dugay
Jim Dureen
Randy Doorman
Bruce Edgeley
Jim Edwards
George Elmes
Gary English
Gerry Enright
Gary Evans
John Fletcher
Bob Foster
Ron Frew
Ron Ferguson
George Fordeska
Jim Forsyth

Roch Gauthier
Toney Gagne.
Ray Gill
Teresa Gowans
Paul Greenhaigh
Al Gjestrm
Al Hadvick
Bubba Hakeem
Steve Hall
Dave Hammer
Bill Harsant
Nigel Harper
Ken Hassel
Blair Henry
Don Havlin
Shawn Hicky
Joe Hills
Ralph Heartland
Ed Holigroski
Grant Hostetter
Walt Hovey
Butch Howes
Daryl Huff
Lee Hundseth
Roger Jacobson
Wayne King
Jack Kobayashi
Tom Ladoucer
Serg Lavoie
Jim Lowzenchuk
Brenda Marshall
Fred Martin
Dwayne McLeod
Jim Mackie
Colin McKenzie
Michel McRae
Bob Montgomery
Dick Moran
Quinn Mobesius
Rod Mullin

George Nelmes
Alfrey Nordal
Dana Odell
Jim Oslund
Rick Oslund
Ron Osborne
Bruce Pachinski
Andy Paradis
Pete Peterson
Wayne Peeke
Brian Poxon
Jay Puff
Herb Reynett
Lolllita, Rocheleau Lazenby
Al Serdar
Ron Schroeder
Denis Schnider
Ken Sissons
Jean Smith
Jack Sonmor
John Tarala
Toney Teunissen
Norm Thomas
Colin Thompson
Rollie Villarica
Ken Virk
Fran Wright
Gary Young
Roy Yasuda
George York

CONCLUSION

Working in jail changes a person. When I retired, my dream was to apply to be a staff training officer at the regional staff college. I really wanted to pass on my knowledge and experience to new and up-and-coming recruits. But in the end it was not to be, as the CSC decided to combine their staff training facilities and move to Ontario.

People ask me how I survived working for corrections for over 36 years, so I tell them simply this.

The job that we do is not like any other job that the public knows. It does, however, come with a cost, and that cost is simple.

We see things most people will never see in their lifetime—death, extreme violence, hangings, stabbings, riots, fellow officers being seriously injured or killed, or worse yet, they commit suicide. As a result, I have personally known officers who have taken their own lives, and other officers who suffer every day from PTSD.

Working at Kent during the mid-80s, I don't think there was a week that I did not come home with blood on my uniform. Lucky for me, it was never my own. In my day, we learned to hide our emotions, to box them up and bury them deep within ourselves. I am sure there are many who are in the system to this day who knows this to be true, and many who also have issues dealing with the day-to-day incidents within those four walls.

I am of the old guard school, officers who believe in honour and code, and in looking after my fellow officers and watching their backs. As I have previously stated, it's not our job to judge inmates. That was already done by a jury of their peers. It is our job to protect the Canadian public, as well as protecting the inmates from harming one another, and to protect public property. Back in my day, we depended on one another for support and comradeship. We are, and will always be, brothers and sisters. The bonds we shared walking those tiers together will never be forgotten, and it is that mutual bond and support that got us through some pretty tough times. No matter what, we had each other's backs.

It takes a special breed of person to work in a prison, but just like any other place of work, you will find the good along with the bad. Over the years, I have worked alongside many outstanding officers, male and female, who think with their heads rather than with their bronze.

> "Nearly all men can stand adversity, but if you want to test a man's character give him power."

> —Abraham Lincoln

End.

ACKNOWLEDGEMENTS

To the Canadian Armed Forces: Thank you for the training and for teaching me what it truly means to serve one's country.

To the Correctional Service of Canada: Thank you for a challenging career.

To Joy: Thank you for your support.

To retired Commissioner of Corrections Don Head: Thank you for everything we achieved together during our contract negotiations.

To retired UCCO-SACC-CSN National Advisor Michel Gauthier: Thank you for your support and knowledge and your understanding, especially through the difficult times.

To the late Tom Croizer: Thank you for all that we achieved while you were Warden of Elbow Lake Institution.

To retired Warden Doug Black: Thank you for your leadership and support.

To retired Warden Judy Croft: Thank you for your leadership and your compassion.

To retired Warden Hilda Frye: Thank you for your support and open door policy, which allowed us to make Kwìkwèxwelhp Healing Village a safe and enjoyable workplace.

To Grace Reagh: Thank you for taking the time to read my first manuscript and helping me edit it.

To the many men and women who are correctional officers today, and those who are retired.

REFERENCES

Blanco, Juan Ignacio. "Clifford Robert Olson." *Murderpedia* (2017). https://murderpedia.org/male.O/o/olson-clifford-robert.htm

"Elbow has first escape of the year." *The Chilliwack Progress* (May 30, 2000).

Falkenberg, Mark. "Elbow Lake Escapees Sought in Murder of Chilliwack Man." *The Chilliwack Progress* (May 4, 1999).

Falkenberg, Mark. "Second Murder Suspect Arrested." *The Chilliwack Progress* (May 19, 1999).

Freeman, Robert. "Living a nightmare." *The Chilliwack Progress* (February 27, 1991).

Government of Canada. "Institutional Profiles: Pacific Region: Mountain Institution." *Correctional Service Canada* (September 12, 2017): http://www.csc-scc.gc.ca/institutions/001002-5007-eng.shtml

Government of Canada. "Kent Institution." *Parole Board of Canada* (February 28, 2020): https://www.canada.ca/en/parole-board/corporate/publications-and-forms/federal-institutions/pacific-region/kent-institution.html

Gray, Ron. "Rain Cools Inmates After Riot." *The Chilliwack Progress* (June 10, 1981).

Hall, Shawn. "Blessing the Longhouse." *The Chilliwack Progress* (October 28, 2001).

Hard Time [Booklet] (Montreal, QC: UCCO-SACC-CSN, 2004).

Jackson, Michael. "*McCann v. The Queen*, 1975 – The 'Cruel and Unusual Punishment' Case." *Justice Behind the Walls: A Study of the Disciplinary Process in a Canadian Penitentiary* (Madeira Park, BC: Douglas & McIntyre, 2002).

Mallette, Michelle. "Kent on 'Lockdown' Following Riot." *The Chilliwack Progress* (January 27, 1988).

Mulgrew, Ian. "Clifford Olson – Canada's National Monster – dead at 71." *Vancouver Sun* (October 10, 2011): http://www.vancouversun.com/news/Clifford+Olson+Canada+national+monster+dead/5484826/story.html

"Prisoners Sentenced." *The Chilliwack Progress*, April 12, 1995.

Province of British Columbia. "Wildfire Crews." *Public Safety and Emergency Services* (2020):

https://www2.gov.bc.ca/gov/content/safety/wildfire-status/about-bcws/wildfire-response/response/crews

Scott, Jack David. *Four Walls in the West: The Story of the British Columbia Penitentiary* (Retired Federal Prison Officers Association of British Columbia, 1984).

"Stabbing Death Draws Murder Charges for Two Elbow Lake Prisoners. The Chilliwack Progress (October 12, 1994).

"The Vancouver Declaration on Human Settlements." UN Habitat – The Vancouver Declaration, 1976 (June 17, 2016), http://habitat76.ca/2016/06/united-nations-habitat-i-vancouver-declaration-1976/

UCCO SACC CSN | Union of Canadian Correctional Officers (2020): https://ucco-sacc-csn.ca/.

Wikipedia, s.v. "Edward VIII," last modified September 10, 2020, 18:57, https://en.wikipedia.org/wiki/Edward_VIII

Wikipedia, s.v. "HMCS *Gatineau* (DDE 236)," last modified September 8, 2019, 13_18, https://en.wikipedia.org/wiki/HMCS_Gatineau_(DDE_236)

"Wonnacott captured." *The Chilliwack Progress* (May 14, 1999).

CPSIA information can be obtained
at www.ICGtesting.com
Printed in the USA
LVHW071946090221
678648LV00038B/1166